Righting of Wrongs

The Story of Esther and Mordecai

A.J. Lykosh

MAKARIOS
PRESS

Esmont, VA

Makarios Press
P.O. Box 28, Esmont, VA 22937

Scripture in NIV unless otherwise stated.

Cover Illustration: Jonelle Lilly
Design: Nate Braxton

ISBN 978-1-956561-32-6

Printed in the United States of America

HIDDEN

The name of God does not appear in Esther.
But take note.

Five times in Esther, in acrostics,[1]
The name of God appears.

Hidden,
But present.

Four times, the name transliterated
    Yahweh, Jehovah:
YHVH.

And once the name God speaks to Moses, "I am
    that I am":
EHYH.

Moses promised that when the Israelites fell away,
God would be hidden from them.[2]

God was hidden from them, the book of
    Esther shows:
They were not hidden from God.[3]

CONTENTS

INTRODUCTION

I didn't want to write a book about Esther.

In my circles, I felt like every time I turned around, someone was breathlessly declaring, "For such a time as this!"

And while I appreciate the general idea that God gives each one of us a unique place and role in the kingdom, the quote started to feel like a Christian cliché.

Was that really the Lord's invitation to me? Write about a statement I thought was overused and abused?

Not only that (and this pains me to admit), but I thought I already knew the story of Esther. Quite well, actually!

But the invitation was clear, so reluctantly I began.

Had I refused, I would have missed out on so much.

I knew the story of Esther in broad strokes, but before writing, I had missed the intensity of the palace politics, the overwhelming task facing Esther, and the true glory of Mordecai.

As soon as I finished the first draft, I wanted to share about it ... and keep sharing.

Changing topics: I like free verse poetry because it allows the story to move along rapidly without sacrificing emotion.

One reader commented, "I've never read anything like this. I just read 40 pages in five minutes ... and I think I'm okay with that!"

Another said, "I get a *selah* moment, a holy pause, on every page. So even though your book isn't long, it takes me a while to get through, because there's so much richness."

Amen! I love that! Both the fast readers and the slow

savorers!

In this book, I footnote when I quote a specific verse. When a quote has no footnote, it's my own translation, created from a combination of a Hebrew interlinear Bible, multiple translations (so thankful for Bible Hub, which offers each verse in about thirty translations), commentaries, lexicons.

And sanctified imagination.

I invite you, too, to come and witness this familiar story with new eyes.

— AJ Lykosh

BEFORE

The Jews

The Patriarchs followed God:
Abraham,
Isaac,
Jacob.

Jacob, called Israel,
Had twelve sons.
These formed the twelve tribes of Israel.

Enslavement in Egypt.
Exodus.
Wandering in the wilderness.
Conquest of the promised land.
Saul.
David.
Solomon.

Then division.
Ten tribes to the north: Israel.

Two tribes to the south, including
    Jerusalem: Judah.

Israel, without even one godly king to lead, fell to
    the Assyrians first.[4]
Judah, with a scattered few godly kings, fell to the
    Babylonians later.[5]

In captivity, the Babylonians shortened the name
    of their conquered people
From "Judah,"
To the single syllable, "Jew."

The Babylonians, in their turn, fell to the Medes
    and Persians,
Which is where this story began,
At the Persian Court in Susa.[6]

Chronology

In the Old Testament,
Four books about God's people in exile.

Read from front to back, the first, Ezra,
Details the rebuilding of the temple.

The second, Nehemiah,
Details the need to rebuild the wall of Jerusalem.

The third, Esther,
Tells the story of how the Jews avoided genocide.

The fourth, Daniel,
Tells stories and dreams from the king's court
   in Babylon.

These have their places for a reason:
The temple holds pre-eminence over the wall.

Male-centric stories
Come before female.

Daniel counts as prophecy more than history,
And so comes in the collection of major prophets.

But to keep chronology clear,
The books in order by date:

Daniel,
Esther,
Nehemiah,
Ezra.[7]

A Warning

Almost a thousand years before Esther and the
  children of Israel
Found themselves in Susa,
At the end of Moses' life,[8]
The Lord said to him:

"You are going to rest with your ancestors,
And these people will soon
Prostitute themselves
To the foreign gods
Of the land they are entering.

They will forsake me
And break the covenant I made with them.

And in that day
I will become angry with them
And forsake them;

I will hide my face from them,
And they will be destroyed.
Many disasters and calamities will come on them,
And in that day they will ask,

'Have not these disasters come on us
Because our God is not with us?'

And I will certainly
Hide my face
In that day
Because of all their wickedness in turning to
    other gods."[9]

PART ONE
TRAGEDY

SCENE 1

The Opening Words of the Book

"Now it came to pass."

In the Hebrew, this specific phrase appears
Six times in the scriptures.
Six: the number of man.
Each time it marks
A time of trouble ending in blessing.

First: various kings rose up against other kings,
Until Abraham's nephew Lot was taken.
Abraham pursued and defeated,
And as he returned, Melchizedek, king of Salem,
    king of peace, blessed him.[10]

Second: Naomi and family went to Moab,
Where her husband and sons died. Bitter,
    she returned.
Widowed daughter-in-law Ruth returned with her.
New husband, new child, new hope: King David

will ascend soon.[11]

Third: during the time of King David, famine
    stalked the land.
The hidden cause: a broken vow.
Retribution demanded and given,
Until "God again answered prayer in behalf of
    the land."[12]

Fourth: here,
At the start of the book of Esther.

Fifth: the king of Israel rose up against the
    king of Judah,
And the people of Judah thought they
    had no hope.
But always hope: "The LORD himself will give
    you a sign:
The virgin will conceive and bear a son, and will
    call him Immanuel."[13]

Sixth: the prophet Jeremiah, writing as the
    children of Israel
Prepared to go into exile.
But the LORD declared to him: "They will fight
    against you
But will not overcome you, for I am with you and
    will rescue you."[14]

At the Start

"Now it came to pass in the days of Ahasuerus,
(This is Ahasuerus which reigned,
From India even unto Ethiopia,
Over an hundred and seven and twenty
   provinces.)"[15]

At the start: a king,
And the extent of his kingdom.

From his palace in the Middle East,
In today's Iran,

The king ruled from South Asia
To the Horn of Africa,
"The two extreme boundaries
Of the known world."[16]

For the Historian

Of the several kings
Who held the title "Ahasuerus,"

The book of Esther features
The one with 127 provinces.

Ahasuerus. The Venerable King.

Not a name like "George Washington,"
But a title like "President."

Proper name: "Astyages" in Greek,
"Arsames" in Persian.

A Sense of Time and Place

Three years into his reign, the king threw a party
At Susa, the capital of the Persian Empire.

Today these abandoned ruins
Sit on the river Shapur, east of the Persian Gulf.

Shock and Awe

Today, marketers emphasize
The need for shock and awe—
Astonish potential customers
With all that you can do.

In the days of Ahasuerus,
He was already practicing this principle.
He gave a banquet for all his nobles and officials,
Plus the military leaders, the power of Persia
    and Media.

For a full 180 days, he displayed
The riches of his glorious kingdom,
And the splendor and glory of his majesty,
As the parade of people passed before him.

Stand astonished.
Remember your place.

The Local Party

When the six months of feasting finished,
And the guests returned home,
The king was ready to relax.

He called for a seven-day banquet
For the palace people to celebrate.

Come, all, to the palace garden!
Great and small! And welcome to you!

The Palace Garden

The unnamed author wrote with
Intimate knowledge of the people and places.

Observe the details of the palace garden
In the citadel of Susa.

Hangings of pale cotton and amethyst,
Held in lines of fine linen and purple,
Tied to silver rings on marble pillars.

Recline on couches of gold and silver,
Resting on a mosaic pavement of
Red porphyry with its feldspar-crystals,
Marble and black marble,
Mother-of-pearl,
And other costly stones.

Drinks flowed with abandon from the
    abundance of wine,
Wine as abundant as the hand of the king,
Served in golden goblets,
Each unique.

You've been working hard.
Now celebrate!

Disconcerting Foreshadowing

"By the king's command
Each guest was allowed to drink
With no restrictions,
For the king instructed
All the wine stewards
To serve each man what he wished."[17]

On the surface, a straightforward statement.
The king wanted everyone to have a good time,
And gave instruction to his people to make
   it happen.

And yet ...

The words, "By the king's command,"
Obscure the meaning:

Law,
Royal decree,
Mandate,
Edict.

The same word used for
One of the laws of the Persians and Medes
That cannot be repealed.[18]

The king issued a royal edict regarding ...

Wine.
What kind of juvenile, foolish court is this?

Laws ought to be serious systems of justice,
Not trivial whims.

The irrational behavior had only begun.

At the Same Time

So often the women in the scriptures go unnamed.
But the first female mentioned in this book
   goes by name:

Vashti the queen,
Who hosted a feast for the women in the
   royal house.

History records that she was
Daughter of the king of Lydia,

Royal by birth
And upbringing.

A Simple Instruction

On the seventh day of the feast,
When the king was in high spirits from the wine,
He instructed his seven eunuchs,
Each mentioned by name—
Mehuman, Biztha, Harbona, Bigtha, and Abagtha,
    Zethar, and Carcas—

To bring Queen Vashti to him,
Royal crown on her head.
Lovely to look on.

Let her display her beauty to the guests.

Denied

In response to the king's edict,
Vashti refused to come.

Curious Behavior

More than two millennia after the royal snub,
The question continues:

Why would Vashti say no to her drunken husband,
In front of his friends?

She not only dishonored and shamed him,
But he was in no rational frame of mind to receive
   this well.

Was she offended by the eunuchs as the delivery
   mechanism?
Was she too proud to be seen by the guests,
   especially the less important?
Was she, royal by birth, a bit too stuck up for
   her own good?
Was she having too good a time with the women
   and couldn't be bothered?
Or perhaps she had been around too many
   drunken parties and she couldn't stomach
   another one?
What if she was an introvert, and 187 days of
   parties really was beyond the limit?
Or is there, implied, the idea that she should
   come, clothed with royal crown ... and
   nothing else?
Or, perhaps, she objected to being displayed, as a

living equivalent to the various riches that had
already been displayed during the 180 days?

No way to know for sure.

This simple request, denied, set in motion
massive action.

Furious

When Vashti disobeyed his word,
The king, furious, burned with anger.

He turned then to his seven closest advisors,
Those highest in the kingdom,
Seven princes of Persia and Media,
All mentioned by name—
Carshena, Shethar, Admatha, Tarshish, Meres,
  Marsena, and Memukan—

To determine his next step.

Wise Men

The seven advisors
Knew the times.

In I Chronicles 12:32, we read of the men
    of Issachar,
"Men who understood the times and knew what
    Israel should do."

The scripture says of both the Persian advisors
And the men of Issachar

The same words:
"Knew the times."

But the men of Issachar had one additional word:
"Understanding."

Not enough to simply know.
Anyone could do that.

Without understanding,
Be prepared for bad judgment.

With wise men like these to advise,
Who needs enemies?

How to Proceed?

The king asked his experts in
Law and judgment,
Those who knew the legal code
And legal pleas:

"According to the law of the Persians and Medes,
What must be done to Queen Vashti?
She has not obeyed the command of King
    Ahasuerus
That the eunuchs have taken to her."[19]

No Sense of Proportion

Memukan answered the king:

"Queen Vashti has done wrong,
Not only against the king,
But also against all the nobles and the peoples
Of all the provinces of King Ahasuerus.

For the queen's conduct will become known to all
    the women,
And so they will despise their husbands and say,
'King Ahasuerus commanded Queen Vashti to be
    brought before him,
But she would not come.'

This very day the Persian and Median women of
    the nobility
Who have heard about the queen's conduct
Will respond to all the king's nobles in the
    same way.
There will be no end of disrespect and discord."[20]

Is Memukan correct?

On the one hand, refusing a royal summons does
    seem imprudent,
A snub from wife and embarrassment to husband,
A bit of marital discord on public display.

On the other hand, we're talking about a
    drunken request
For a public showing,
Not the massacre of the innocents.

Wasn't this a tempest in a teacup?

Thinking About Group Think

Who has been tempted
To copy the bad behavior of royals
After hearing rumors about it?

Was Memukan's assumption correct,
That now all women would despise
    their husbands,
Even as Vashti did?

Is not respect founded on being a person of honor,
Worthy of esteem? No palace intrigue
Should be able to dislodge appropriate regard.

The Next Law

Memukan proposed that the king
Issue another edict.

"Since your edict summoning Vashti
Took no effect,

This time issue an edict,
And also let it be written

In the laws of Persia and Media,
Which cannot be repealed,

That Vashti is never again
To enter the presence of the king."

Let the punishment fit the crime.
She didn't want to come to the king?

Very well.
Let her never come before him again.

Forced absence,
Extending to the farthest possible extreme.

Replacement

After Vashti's eviction,
"Let the king give her royal position
To someone else who is better than she."

Reasonable advice.

The king had appetites.
Find a way to satisfy the appetites
With someone more tractable.

"Then when the king's sentence is proclaimed
Throughout all his vast realm,
All the women will respect their husbands,
From the least to the greatest."

Unreasonable advice.

Though wives may have feared their husbands,
And earnestly hoped not to be discarded,
Respect cannot be gained by force.

Respect can be offered and desired, but not
    commanded.

Like love.

Flattery

Memukan knew how to manipulate.

Like a good marketer,
His words assumed the king was on board
    with his plan.

Not, "*If* the king's sentence is proclaimed,"
But "*when.*"

No apparent question that he could make the king
    do his bidding.

And note the subtle flattery:

"When the king's sentence is proclaimed
Throughout *all his vast realm.*"

Oh, king, you have such territory!
Such responsibility!
How powerful you are!

Beware the flatterer.

God at Work in the House of the King

Throughout the book of Esther,
No one speaks the name of God.[21]

Hundreds of years before, God said to Moses,
"I will certainly hide my face in that day,"
Because of all the wickedness of the children
    of Israel,
Turning to other gods

God, indeed, hid his face.

But this is not the full story.

When Memukan said,
"All the wives shall give
To their husbands honor,"

The initial letters of these words in Hebrew
Form an acrostic,
Spelling out the name of God ...
But in reverse.

Not YHVH,
But HVHY.

As if, in order to write the acronym "LORD,"
The author wrote:
"Due Respect Our Ladies
Shall give to their husbands."[22]

Memukan the Gentile
Spoke words concerning a queen.
Initial letters initiated an event,
And the words formed God's name backward,
For God would turn back and overrule
The counsels of man.

Pleased

"The king and his nobles
Were pleased with this advice,
So the king did as Memukan proposed.

He sent dispatches to all parts of the kingdom,
To each province in its own script
And to each people in their own language,

Proclaiming that every man should be ruler
Over his own household,
Using his native tongue."[23]

SCENE 2

A Truism

"Marry in haste, repent at leisure."

Ahasuerus divorced in haste,
Then repented at leisure.

He remembered the beautiful Vashti.

But the law was the law,
And could not be repealed.

Project: Queen Replacement

Unhappy kings have never been good for
Health and head of advisors.

"The king's personal attendants proposed,
'Let a search be made for beautiful young virgins
　　for the king.
Let the king appoint commissioners in every
　　province of his realm
To bring all these beautiful young women into
　　the harem
At the citadel of Susa.
Let them be placed under the care of Hegai, the
　　king's eunuch,
Who is in charge of the women;
And let beauty treatments be given to them.
Then let the young woman who pleases the king
　　be queen instead of Vashti.'
This advice appealed to the king, and he
　　followed it."[24]

No mention made of what the young
　　men of Persia
Thought of all the beautiful virgins of the land
Going to live in the king's harem.

What a way to get a wife.

Introducing Mordecai

Mordecai,
A Jew of the tribe of Benjamin,

Son of Jair,
Son of Shimei,
Son of Kish,
Dwelled in the citadel at Susa.

Nebuchadnezzar king of Babylon had carried him
From Jerusalem into exile,
Among those taken captive with Jehoiachin king
    of Judah.[25]

The Tribe of Benjamin

The generations of the Jews matter.
Benjamin, "son of my right hand,"
Youngest son of Jacob,
Second son born to his favorite wife Rachel.
Rachel died after giving birth to Benjamin.
A welcome son, but a grievous entrance.

A small tribe.
In the days of Judges,
"Israel had no king;
Everyone did as they saw fit."[26]

And the tribe of Benjamin behaved so badly,
The other tribes rose up to kill them all.
They almost succeeded.

Six hundred Benjamites hid in a cave for
     four months.
When they emerged,
First the rest of the tribes vowed
"Not one of us will give his daughter in marriage
     to a Benjamite."[27]
That settled, they went to Bethel, the
     house of God,
And wept.
"Why should one tribe be missing from
     Israel today?"[28]

To repopulate the desolate,
The tribes then killed all the men of
  Jabesh Gilead,
The only city that failed to muster with the others,
The only city that failed to take the vow.
Only four hundred unmarried women dwelled
  there, though.

And so the people instructed the two hundred
  Benjamites still in need of wives
To hide in vineyards during a festival.
"When the young women of Shiloh come out to
  join in the dancing,
Rush from the vineyards and each of you seize one
  of them to be your wife.
Then return to the land of Benjamin.
When their fathers or brothers complain to us, we
  will say to them,
'Do us the favor of helping them,
Because we did not get wives for them
  during the war.
You will not be guilty of breaking your oath
Because you did not give your daughters
  to them.'"[29]

What a way to repopulate a place.[30]

What a way to get a wife.

Kish

Soon after the tiny, almost annihilated tribe of
  Benjamin began to rebuild,
Kish the Benjamite
Fathered Saul, first king over the children of Israel.[31]

Another descendant of Kish,
Shimei by name,
Later cursed David as he fled from his son Absalom.
Appalled, David's attendants asked if Shimei should
  be killed.
David refused.

Perhaps Shimei was speaking the words of God.
Who could say?[32]

Later, after David's throne was restored to him,
Shimei repented.[33]
David agreed not to kill him,
But, as part of his deathbed charge to
  Solomon his son,
He again mentioned Shimei's treachery.[34]

Solomon summoned Shimei,
Restricted his travel as punishment,
And, some time later, when Shimei went too
  far afield,
His life was forfeit.[35]

Faithfulness

The generations of Mordecai—
And of all of us—
Depend not on human faithfulness,
But God's.

Good thing.

Introducing Esther

Mordecai took his cousin for his own daughter,
After her father Abihail and her mother died.

"Hadassah" in Hebrew,
"Esther" in Persian,

Beautiful in face and form.

Abihail

Esther's father's name means
"My father is might."

Not true of her earthly father, who left
  her orphaned.
But completely, absolutely, entirely true of her
  heavenly Father.

In Hebrew

"Hadassah," in Hebrew, means
"Myrtle":

A fragrant, evergreen shrub
With small, glossy green leaves,
White, star-shaped flowers,
And, after blooming, purple-black berries,
Useful for healing.

The glorious prophecy of Isaiah 55 ends
With a reversal:
From brier to myrtle.

"You will go out in joy and be led forth in peace;
The mountains and hills will burst into song
   before you,
And all the trees of the field will clap their hands.
Instead of the thornbush will grow the juniper,
And instead of briers the myrtle will grow.
This will be for the Lord's renown,
For an everlasting sign,
That will endure forever."[36]

In Persian

"Esther," in Persian, means
"Star":

A light in the darkness,
A spark of beauty.

The glorious hymn of praise of Psalm 8 opens
With a celebration of creation:
From stars to man.

"Lord, our Lord,
How majestic is your name in all the earth!
You have set your glory
In the heavens.
Through the praise of children and infants
You have established a stronghold against
   your enemies,
To silence the foe and the avenger.
When I consider your heavens,
The work of your fingers,
The moon and the stars,
Which you have set in place,
What is mankind that you are mindful of them,
Human beings that you care for them?"[37]

Taken

The king's word and the king's irrevocable law
Went forth,
And the young women were brought together
To the palace of Susa.

Esther, too, was taken,
And entrusted to Hegai,
In charge of the women.

Logistics

No mention made of how this
Bringing and taking
Took place, practically.

Did young women volunteer for this,
Lining up as in a pageant, eager for a life of ease in
    the palace?

Or were they hunted down and kidnapped?

Was it a sign of honor to be selected?
Or a horror to hide from, a grief to be picked?

Practically

Looking back from the space of more than two
      millennia,
It seems a grim fate for all singled out and chosen:

Enter the palace and never leave again.
Have one night as the plaything of the king,
Who has given no indication that he would have
Any concern or sympathy for the pain or
      discomfort of the first time.

Perhaps you'll be chosen,
But the odds are not in your favor.

Spend the rest of your life
Surrounded by women in the house of
      the also-ran,
The rejected and lonely, the childless and bored,
Names forgotten,
With all the cattiness and hormones of a
      sorority house.

Unsung Hero

In Esther's childhood, Mordecai took her in.
But when he could no longer care for her,

Hegai the eunuch took over the responsibility
For her welfare.

Esther pleased him,
And won his favor.

He gave her beauty treatments
And special food,

Along with seven attendants
And the best place in the house of women.

What could have been a disorienting
   transition was

Protected.

She Obtained Kindness

Esther "obtained kindness" of Hegai.[38]
She "won his favor."

The word translated "kindness" or "favor"
Is the Hebrew word *hesed*, or *chesed*,
Translated elsewhere

Mercy.
Kindness.
Goodness.
Faithfulness.

Lovingkindness.

No English Equivalent

Translation gives such gifts,
Allowing thoughts from one culture
To cross
To another culture.

But some words have no equivalent,
And require rich study
To tease out meanings.

Like the Hebrew *hesed*,
Whose root word means:
"To bow one's head toward another,"
Particularly in a covenant relationship.[39]

In English, combined words
    approximate meaning:
Loyal-love.
Steadfast-love.
Faithful-love.
Unfailing-love.[40]

Think:
"Ardent desire for someone,
Zeal toward a person,
Or abiding favor."[41]

Or:

"Tenderness and consideration ...
Always towards others....
An outward expression,
Not one of self-seeking motivation."[42]

"Hesed is never merely an abstract feeling of
   goodwill,
But always entails practical action on behalf of
   another."[43]

It "intervenes on behalf of loved ones
And comes to their rescue."[44]

From Beginning to End

Hesed shows up 251 times
In the Old Testament,
From beginning to end.

The first when Lot, overwhelmed by the trouble
Coming upon Sodom and Gomorrah,
Pleaded with his two guests (or hosts):

"Your servant has found favor in your eyes,
And you have shown great *kindness* to me in
    sparing my life.
But I can't flee to the mountains; this disaster will
    overtake me, and I'll die."[45]

The last when the prophet Zechariah proclaimed,
"This is what the LORD Almighty said:
    'Administer true justice;
Show *mercy* and compassion to one another.'"[46]

Also in Micah's beautiful summary of
    approved action:
"He has shown you, O mortal, what is good.
And what does the LORD require of you?

To act justly
And to love *mercy*
And to walk humbly with your God."[47]

And in David's famous song of
The LORD as his shepherd,
He ends: "Surely your goodness

And *love*
Will follow me all the days of my life,
And I will dwell in the house of the LORD
     forever."[48]

Goodness and lovingkindness *follow* David.
Not as a gentle puppy follows,
A bit bewildered and easily distracted,

But *follow* as a predator intent on its prey.
Goodness and lovingkindness tracking him down.
Inexorable. Inescapable.

One of God's Attributes

God spoke his name to Moses.
But "name" in Hebrew was not simply
The word to call someone.

One's name implied
Nature, character, authority, honor, renown.[49]

And *hesed*, lovingkindness,
Has always been part of God's name, nature,
  character.

When God spoke his name, he began:

"The LORD, the LORD,
The compassionate and gracious God,
Slow to anger,
Abounding in *love* and faithfulness,
Maintaining *love* to thousands,
And forgiving wickedness, rebellion and sin."[50]

Show *hesed* and be godlike.

Cocooned

Esther, first orphaned,
Now transplanted into the king's harem.
So protected, with the eunuch's
Lovingkindness
Caring for her.

Mordecai, too, continued his care:
"Every day he walked back and forth
Near the courtyard of the harem
To find out how Esther was
And what was happening to her."[51]

And so she continued to live,
Surrounded by a cocoon of kindness.

Hidden

Though Esther's Persian name means "star,"
In Hebrew, it might come from *sathar*,

To hide.[52]

When Esther entered the palace,
Mordecai charged her
Not to reveal her people,
Nor her kindred.

She concealed her nationality
And her family background.

Thus forbidden,
She stayed hidden.

Dodging Bureaucracy

Think how much goes unsaid.
A single verse hides an untold story.

Could Persian bureaucracy be much different
Than ours today?

Think of endless forms: name, nationality, family
  background.

Think of the questions Esther would have
   had to dodge
From officials, competitors,
The responsible, the bored, and the curious.

Not enough for Mordecai to simply say, "I forbid
   you to speak"—
She would have needed
Some story to tell,
And constant vigilance to keep her true
   self secret.

She was not, after all, a cipher until she showed up
At the citadel in Susa.

Wisdom

What foresight of Mordecai.
What wisdom.

Already note the sharp contrast

Between this hidden wise man
And the shortsighted advisors and their
    foolish king.

Obedience

What resourcefulness of Esther.
What obedience.

Already note the sharp contrast

Between this hidden obedient maiden
And the refractory Vashti.

The First Six Months

Treatments with oil of myrrh:

Kills harmful bacteria.
Supports oral health.
Boosts skin health and heals any sores.
Fights pain and swelling—including headaches.
Possibly an antioxidant, to prevent aging.
Kills parasites.
Improves gut health.[53]

In an era without
Antibiotics,
Immunizations,
Toothpaste and toothbrushes,
Topical steroids,
Probiotics,
And so on—

This was a good way to prevent harm
To the women, and especially

To the king.

The Next Six Months

Perfumes to smell as good as possible.
Cosmetics to look as good as possible.

Most likely also things like
Massage and depilation.

Anything to create
The most desirable, alluring female.

After That Year

Finally finished with the beauty treatments,
Each woman waited her turn
For the pivotal evening to morning.

On her day,
She would pack her things,
As she would not be returning again.

Though not quite the story of
Shahrazad and the 1001 Arabian Nights—
No woman awaited death the next day—

She was cut off from the other virgins,
And transplanted from the harem
To the house of the concubines.

"She would not return to the king
Unless he was pleased with her
And summoned her by name."[54]

Satiation

What a distasteful method of spouse selection.

If you're good enough in bed for me to remember
    your name ...
Maybe we'll see each other again.

How much of that one night encounter would
    depend on chance:
How tired was the king?
How grumpy from the cares of the day?
Did his body ache in any way?
Did he eat too much at dinner?

Surrounded by all the woman he could
    possibly desire—
Literally—

What could one virgin do to make a lasting
    impression
On this powerful man
Who holds her future
By the slender thread of a

Single
Night.

In Turn

No mention that a new virgin went to the king
   each night.
Presumably he called for one when he was ready.

No mention of how their turns were chosen.
If the order went by arrival, Esther, as a local girl,
   would have been early.

Or maybe the selection was at Hegai's discretion.
Would he post the list at the start of each week,
   showing who's on deck?
Or pick each time, based on the court gossip of
   the king's mood?

You wouldn't want to be first,
As you'd be fighting the king's curiosity about
   what might yet come.

But don't wait too long:
Any day, the king might choose his queen.

The Day

When Esther's turn came,
She asked for nothing other than what Hegai
    suggested.

As with Mordecai, once again she demonstrated
    her willingness
To listen to her advisor,
To trust his judgment,
To be obedient,
To reject any tendency to willfulness.

Favor

"And Esther won the favor of everyone who
   saw her."[55]

Here, the word *favor* is not the *hesed*
   "lovingkindness."
This "favor" is *hen*:

Grace, charm, elegance, acceptance.
Well-favored. Pleasant, precious, gracious.

Subjective kindness,
Objective beauty.

Because of her beauty and grace,
Other people were beautiful and graceful
   toward her.

Four Years Later

The king threw his half-year party in the third year
    of his reign,
Probably ending right around the start of his
    fourth year.

Perhaps it took a few months for his anger to cool,
    for him to miss Vashti.
Let's imagine it is fourth year, sixth month.

Then a year for finding maidens,
Scouring the kingdom for the young beauties. Fifth
    year, sixth month.

A full year of beauty treatments then,
Until the sixth year, sixth month.

Esther's turn comes in the seven year, tenth month[56].
A long time to wait.

A long time for those in the harem.
A long time for Mordecai, trying to get his
    daily report.

A long time for the advisors, waiting for the shame of
    their Vashti plan to fade.
A long time for the king, now queen-less for
    four years.

Queen

"Now the king was attracted to Esther
More than to any of the other women,

And she won his favor and approval
More than any of the other virgins.

So he set a royal crown on her head
And made her queen instead of Vashti."[57]

She won both *hen*, his favor, his grace, his
    acceptance,
And *hesed*, his lovingkindness, covenant
    relationship.

From One Protector to Another

The day Esther lost
Hegai her protector,

She gained the king in
That same role.

Hegai offered lovingkindness.
Everyone else offered favor.

In the single person of the king
She found both.

Feast

Four years before, the king "made a feast
Unto all his princes and his servants."[58]

That ended badly.

Now, the same words,
But with one addition:

"The king made a *great* feast
Unto all his princes and his servants,"[59]

Called "Esther's feast."

The former was fine.
But the kingdom now came closer to proper
    alignment:

A great feast, for a better queen.

Also the king proclaimed a holiday throughout
    the provinces,
And distributed gifts with royal generosity.

"When the righteous prosper,
The city rejoices."[60]

The Second Gathering

Immediately following the story of Esther's
  ascension to the throne,
The author wrote: "When the virgins were
  gathered a second time."

Same word for the previous gathering of
  the virgins.
Now, despite his queen, the king apparently called
  for another crop of women.

The author presumably included this as a
  historical time-marker,
As we might say, "When Kennedy was shot."

But this adds an unsettling highlight to Esther's
  precarious place.
Was the king hedging his bets? Keeping
  Esther humble?

So insatiable in sexual drive?
So enjoyed the sense of control over the kingdom?

An unexpected glimpse into the need to
  be on guard.
No trust in this palace.

Still Not the Time
for the Big Reveal

Even after ascending to the throne,
Esther continued to keep secret

Her family background and nationality,
Just as Mordecai had instructed.

She continued to follow Mordecai's commands
As she had done when he was bringing her up.

Earlier, the king commanded Vashti,
To no avail.

Here, Mordecai commanded Esther,
And she obeyed.

Plot and Foil

Bigthan and Teresh guarded the doorway,
But, angered, they conspired to assassinate
   the king.

Mordecai, "sitting at the king's gate,"[61] found out
   about the plot.
He told Queen Esther.

Esther reported it to the king,
Giving credit to Mordecai.

When the report was investigated and found
   to be true,
The two officials were hanged on a tree.

Not a western-style gallows hanging.
That would be anachronistic and incorrect.[62]

But literally affixed in some way
To a pole of wood,

Suspended as a public shaming,
A display for all to see.

Herodotus described impalement as a Persian
   punishment.[63]
Or perhaps it was some sort of crucifixion.

In any case: all this was recorded in the book of
    the annals
In the presence of the king.

Communication

"But Mordecai found out about the plot and told
   Queen Esther,
Who in turn reported it to the king,
Giving credit to Mordecai."[64]

How much this single verse conceals.

How did Mordecai find out?
Presumably the conspirators would not have
   talked loudly of their plans
In public places.
How much risk did he run in the finding?

How did he tell Queen Esther?
Presumably she had very limited access.
Hidden in the palace,
How did she hear?

How did she tell the king?
Presumably she waited until he summoned her.
But what agony in the meantime ...
Hoping the news wouldn't come too late.

The challenge of restricted access:
Unmentioned, but pervasive.

Betrayal

The king's personal bodyguard
Conspired against him.
Personal vendetta.

How unsettling for the king:
Those closest to him,
Ready to betray him.

Who could he trust?

SCENE 3

Backstory Montage of a Long Enmity

After all these things, Ahasuerus promoted
Haman son of Hammedatha,
An Agagite.

Consider the history:

Abraham the Patriarch fathered
Isaac, who fathered twin sons:
Jacob and Esau.

God himself spoke of these brothers:

"'Was not Esau Jacob's brother?' declares the Lord.
'Yet I have loved Jacob,
But Esau I have hated,
And I have turned his hill country into a
    wasteland

And left his inheritance to the desert jackals.'"[65]

Not capricious favoritism,
But a deep grief over this older son
Who loved his appetite and despised his
    birthright,
Who lived his life out of sync with God
    and his ways.

Don't hate the person,
But perhaps hate the spirit a person carries.

Esau's son fathered Amalek.[66]

Many generations later,
The formerly enslaved Israelites had recently
    left Egypt.
They were navigating the challenges of
    desert travel,
When "The Amalekites came and attacked the
    Israelites at Rephidim."[67]
Joshua fought on the plain,
While Moses, Aaron, and Hur watched from the
    hill above.
As long as Moses kept his arms raised, the
    Israelites were winning.

After Joshua defeated the enemy,
"The LORD said unto Moses,
Write this for a memorial in a book,
And rehearse it in the ears of Joshua:
For I will utterly put out the remembrance of
    Amalek from under heaven.
And Moses built an altar,
And called the name of it Jehovah-nissi:

For he said, Because the LORD hath sworn
That the LORD will have war with Amalek
From generation to generation."[68]

Write this on a scroll, and make sure Joshua hears:
"I will completely blot out the name of Amalek
    from under heaven."[69]

About forty years later, when Balak, king of
    the Moabites
Hired Balaam to curse the Israelites,
And Balaam instead proclaimed,
"How beautiful are your tents, Jacob,
Your dwelling places, Israel!"[70]
He also spoke against Amalek:
"Amalek was first among the nations,
But their end will be utter destruction."[71]

Moses, in his farewell address, reminded the
    children of Israel:
"Remember what the Amalekites did to you
Along the way when you came out of Egypt.
When you were weary and worn out,
They met you on your journey
And attacked all who were lagging behind;
They had no fear of God.
When the Lord your God gives you rest from all
    the enemies around you
In the land he is giving you to possess as an
    inheritance,
You shall blot out the name of Amalek from
    under heaven.
Do not forget!"[72]

During the chaotic time of the Judges,

Amalek partnered with other enemies and
   captured Jericho,[73]
And Deborah and Barak sang of victory over
   this enemy.[74]

Then came the time of the kings.

The Downfall of Saul, Israel's First King

Samuel delivered this message to King Saul:
"This is what the Lord Almighty says:
'I will punish the Amalekites
For what they did to Israel
When they waylaid them as they came up
    from Egypt.
Now go, attack the Amalekites and
Totally destroy
All that belongs to them.
Do not spare them;
Put to death men and women,
Children and infants,
Cattle and sheep,
Camels and donkeys.'"[75]

Saul and his men destroyed everything weak
    and despised,
They were unwilling to destroy completely,
But kept alive the best sheep and cattle—

And Agag the king.

"Then the word of the Lord came to Samuel:
'I regret that I have made Saul king,
Because he has turned away from me

And has not carried out my instructions.'
Samuel was angry, and he cried out to the Lord all
    that night."[76]

In the morning, he confronted Saul—
"To obey is better than sacrifice! ...
The Lord has torn the kingdom of Israel from
    you today
And has given it to one of your neighbors—
To one better than you."[77]

And Samuel asked for Agag.

The king of Amalek came before the
    prophet of God,
Thinking, "Surely the bitterness of death is past."

But Samuel said, "As your sword has made women
    childless,
So will your mother be childless among women."

And he put him to death there before
    the LORD.[78]

Jewish tradition, though, records the importance
    of that one extra night:
That Agag raped the servant girl who brought him
    his dinner,
And left a descendant alive, to carry on the war.[79]

His offspring remained.

Epic Showdown

Generations later,

The conflict resumed:
Haman the Agagite,
Descendant of Amalek,[80]
Determined to wipe out
The children of Israel.

And Mordecai,
Descendant of Saul's father,
Determined to protect and guard
Both an orphan of Israel ...

And a foolish king.

Elevation and Prostration

The king magnified
Haman the Agagite,
Elevated above all the other nobles.

All the royal officials at the king's gate
Knelt down and prostrated themselves to Haman,
For so had the king charged.

What had the king charged?

Throughout the Old Testament, we find
    people kneeling:
Sisera, struck down by Jael, knelt in death,[81]
The wife of wicked Phinehas' knelt in grief and
    went into labor,[82]
Solomon knelt before the altar of the LORD,[83]

And most of Israel knelt to the idol Baal.[84]

As for prostration, also translated "worship" and
    "reverence," scores of examples, including
Abraham, before the three men (one of them God
    himself),[85]
The beginning of the Ten Commandments: do not
    bow to idols,[86]
Moses and the elders on the mountain of
    the Lord,[87]

And the children of Israel prostrated themselves
   before the idols of Canaan.[88]

On the surface, perhaps the king's charge
   seems innocent,
A request for courtesy toward his favorite.

But the word choice, mixed with idolatry
   and worship,
Overreached, demanding more than would have
   been right to give.

Insubordination

Mordecai alone did not kneel, nor
    prostrate himself.

Did he know the history of Agag and Amalek?
Did his spirit recoil at the king's charge, sensing
    desecration?

"He could not bow to an Amalekite,
Against whom Jehovah had declared
    perpetual war."[89]

On the one hand, Mordecai hardly seemed a
    likely rebel.
He had lived and worked in the palace—with all
    its intrigues—for years.
His foster daughter competed in—and won—the
    king's sex contest.

On the other hand, his character had never
    shown anything
But alignment with the plumb line of the God
    of heaven.

Of all the palace people, he would be the one
To stand.

Peer Pressure

The other officials asked,
"Why do you disobey the king's charge?"

Asked day
After day.

Mordecai,
Can you please comply?

How important, in a communal culture,
To conform,

Both as a matter of honor to one another,
And as a measure of safety.

This is a volatile king—
Mordecai, your actions could endanger

More
Than just yourself.

To Preempt a Potential Threat

How to deal with a sticky situation?
Go up the chain of command.

Haman had not, apparently, noticed
Mordecai's noncompliance.

Perhaps he was always focused elsewhere.
Presumably Mordecai didn't draw attention to
    himself, not bowing.

Perhaps Mordecai was usually already seated,
And a sitting man looks not much different than
    a bowing man.

But the other officials, whether fearful for
    themselves
Or out of actual dislike, reported Mordecai's
    behavior to Haman.

Scripture records that Mordecai had, at
    some point,
Told the officials that he was a Jew.

It makes no mention of any difference in
    diet or dress.
Assimilated in superficialities, but not in heart.

Fury

Haman, enraged,
Scorned to kill only Mordecai.

No wonder the king liked Haman.

If "Go big or go home" described the king's life,
His parties and his punishments,

Here lived another who shared his
    intemperate appetite.

Haman sought a way to exterminate all the people
    of Mordecai,
All the Jews, throughout the whole kingdom of
    Ahasuerus.

First Month

Five years now from Esther's ascension.

In the twelfth year of the king's reign, in the
    first month,[90]
Haman cast lots for the propitious day to
    destroy the Jews.

The first month is the month of Passover,
And the Feast of First Fruits.

Though Haman did not cast lots on one of
    those days,
He was seeking to overturn and overthrow
    God's gift of

Freedom—Passover—and
Celebration, or Feast—First Fruits.

Cast Lots

Isaiah issued
This warning:

"Keep on, then, with your magic spells
And with your many sorceries,
Which you have labored at since childhood.
Perhaps you will succeed, perhaps you will
    cause terror.

All the counsel you have received has only
    worn you out!
Let your astrologers come forward,
Those stargazers who make predictions month
    by month,
Let them save you from what is coming upon you.

Surely they are like stubble;
The fire will burn them up.
They cannot even save themselves from the power
    of the flame....
There is not one that can save you."[91]

Even had he heard Isaiah's warning,
Haman would not have heeded.

Set in Motion

Once Haman determined the propitious day in
   the twelfth month,[92]
He went to the king to set in motion his carefully
   prepared plot.

"There is a certain people
Dispersed among the peoples in all the provinces
   of your kingdom
Who keep themselves separate.

Their customs are different from those of all
   other people,
And they do not obey the king's laws;
It is not in the king's best interest to tolerate them.

If it pleases the king, let a decree be issued to
   destroy them,
And I will give ten thousand talents of silver
To the king's administrators for the royal
   treasury."[93]

Proxy

"These people keep themselves separate.
They do not assimilate.
And they flout your laws.
Open disregard! Scoff! Mock!"

No record of anyone but Mordecai,
In all the 127 provinces of Ahasuerus,
Defying the laws of the king—
And even Mordecai only defied one law in
    this one way.

Mordecai stood, by proxy,
On behalf of all his people.

But Mordecai: your actions could endanger
More than just yourself.

Cultural Stability

Not easy to understand the importance of
Complete compliance
For cultural stability in the ancient world.

Think of the Romans, ready to destroy a people
    for any cultural breakdown.
Jewish leader Caiaphas, concerned about
    Roman reprisal,
If Jesus, the apparent revolutionary, was permitted
    to continue.
"You do not realize that it is better for you
That one man die for the people
Than that the whole nation perish."[94]

Later, when early Christians in Ephesus
Started to disrupt the social order,
The whole city went into uproar.
A mob shouted for hours until the city clerk
    warned them,
"We are in danger of being charged with rioting
Because of what happened today.
In that case we would not be able to account for
    this commotion,
Since there is no reason for it."[95]
Translation: we don't need the wrath of
    Rome to fall.
Should that happen, none of us might remain!

A charge of separation and disobedience
Was a serious threat to any authoritarian culture.

Ten Thousand Talents

To read the three words "ten thousand talents"
　　takes only a second,
Words that seem no more than a blip in the story.

But Haman offers a staggering sum.

One translation's footnote offers the equivalent:
Haman offered 375 tons of silver.[96]

How to put this in perspective,
As coins and weights fluctuate through time?

Silver is measured in troy ounces,
Slightly heavier than ounces of food.
Haman offered nearly 11 million ounces of silver[97]
In today's measurement.

But even that offers a difficult comparison,
As cultures and mining practices and
　　valuation varies.

More applicable:

In the time of Moses, God demanded a
　　sanctuary tax,
A half shekel per man, twenty years and over,
From the children of Israel.[98]

If an ox gored a servant to death,
The ox owner paid 30 shekels for the replacement
    cost of the servant.[99]

A talent was the equivalent of 3,000
    sanctuary shekels.[100]
Haman offered ten thousand talents:
Thirty million shekels,
The purchase price of one million dead servants.

But even this is a number, easy enough to be
    passed over.

The historian Herodotus, offering a
    delightful mix of
Real and fanciful facts,
Claimed the total income for the Persian Empire
Was 14,460 talents per year.
Most likely this was somewhat inflated.[101]

It seems, then, that Haman was offering roughly
    the equivalent
Of the total income of Persia.[102]

Are your coffers running low, oh, king?
Replenish them, at my expense.

Best Interest

Though the accusation of lack of assimilation
Was possibly a well-founded threat,

The accusation that "it is not in the king's best
    interest to tolerate them"
Was completely wrong.

God told Abraham,
"I will bless those who bless you,
And whoever curses you I will curse;
And all peoples on earth will be blessed
    through you."[103]

It was in the king's best interest not only
    to tolerate,
But also to bless the Jews,

Actually better for the king than ten thousand
    talents of silver.

Truth

Of course, what Haman doesn't mention
Was that he was really talking about
A single man, refusing to bow,
Which he hadn't even noticed
Until others pointed it out to him.

This would be a tempest in a teacup ...
Except that he was an Agagite
With a position of power
And a moment of opportunity.

Open Doors

Why did the king trust Haman
So unreservedly,
To be so incurious as to Haman's target?

Sure, they had similar appetites,
And a wealthy drinking buddy must
    have been fun.

But beyond that, how rare around people of power
To find a companion with such a lack of neediness.

Haman could give to the royal treasury,
And not just take.

Note well.

Whether you wish to destroy
Or rebuild,

Resources
Open
Doors.

Given

The king's signet ring, engraved or embossed,
Pressed into wax, carried the king's authority.

The king took his signet ring from his finger,
And handed it to

Haman, the enemy of the Jews.
No one else in scripture is given that title.

"The silver is given to you, and the people also,
To do with them as seems good to you."

An ambiguous statement to the modern reader.
It sounds like the king was saying,

"Keep your money,
And do what you want with those people."

But later the charge comes that the Jews have
     been sold.
So perhaps the king was saying:

"I give you my ring,
And all the resources required to enact your plan."

The Thirteenth

On the thirteenth day of the first month,
Two days before the Passover celebration,
The royal secretaries were summoned.

In the language and script of each province
   and people,
They wrote all Haman's orders
To the king's lieutenants, governors, and nobles.

In the name of King Ahasuerus was it written,
And sealed with the king's ring,
And sent by runners to all the king's provinces.

Exterminate.
Kill.
Destroy.

On the thirteenth day of the twelfth month,
Utterly annihilate all Jews,
Young and old, women and children.

Need a self-serving reason to do so?
Once they're gone, plan to loot and
Plunder their goods.

A copy of the writing of the law
Went to every province, made known to the

people of every nationality
So they would be ready for that day.
Spurred by the king's word,
The runners went out, carrying
This law of the Persians and Medes that cannot
be repealed.

Outcome

"The king and Haman sat down to drink,
But the city of Susa was bewildered."[104]

The word "bewildered"
Appears only three times in the scripture.

Once here.

Once describing unhappy cattle without pasture,
    lead astray.[105]

Once when Pharaoh said of the Israelites in the
    days of Moses,
"They are entangled in the land."[106]

Turning, rolling, disturbing,
Perplexing, confusing.

Stir up a spring of water,
Leaving a dirty, agitated swirl.

Also: to involve oneself in evil.

Think: stir up a spring of water,
Leaving a dirty, agitated swirl.

The city was troubled, in an uproar,

Thinking confused and unproductive thoughts.

Properly, government is for the punishment of
    evildoers,
And for the praise of them that do well.[107]

Not so here.

"When the righteous thrive, the people rejoice;
When the wicked rule, the people groan."[108]

Cultural Meta-Narrative

In the time of Moses, God had promised
That if his people pursued idols,
He would be angry with them and forsake them.

God had promised to hide his face from them,
So they would be destroyed.
Now the coming destruction appeared to
    be complete.

God had promised that many disasters and
    calamities would come,
So they would ask, "Have not these disasters
    come on us
Because our God is not with us?"

A legitimate question to ask,
And no one to blame but themselves.

They had turned to other gods,
And so God certainly hid his face.

SCENE 4

Outward Signs of Grief

"When Mordecai learned of all that had
   been done,
He tore his clothes,
Put on sackcloth and ashes,
And went out into the city,
Wailing loudly and bitterly.
But he went only as far as the king's gate,
Because no one clothed in sackcloth was allowed
   to enter it

In every province to which the edict and order of
   the king came,
There was great mourning among the Jews,
With fasting, weeping and wailing.
Many lay in sackcloth and ashes."[109]

Death Sentence

Although the text does not make this explicit,
Mordecai must have known why the Jews were
    under sentence of death.

His actions alone sentenced the entire people.

He chose the road of no compromise,
And that led to promised, impending destruction.

Rend your garments, Mordecai.

Anguish

"My God, my God,
Why have you forsaken me?
Why are you so far from saving me,
So far from my cries of anguish?
But you, Lord,
Do not be far from me.
You are my strength;
Come quickly to help me."[110]

The reality:
"For he has not despised or scorned
The suffering of the afflicted one;
He has not hidden his face from him
But has listened to his cry for help."[111]

Signs of Grief

When Patriarch Jacob thought his son Joseph
  was no more,
He tore his clothes and dressed in sackcloth,
A coarse fabric, made from flax or hemp.

Imagine wearing a robe made of twine.

The point is that the discomfort of the skin
  approximates
The pain in the soul.

But though the word "sackcloth" shows up 45
  times in the scriptures,

In many examples of deep grief,

The phrase "sackcloth and ashes" shows up only
  eight times.

First time: Mordecai grieved for his people.[112]
Second time: Jews in Persia grieve, too.[113]
Third time: God asks, sarcastically, if the people
  really thought he desired the sackcloth and ashes
  in the fast.[114]
Fourth time: Jeremiah told the people to mourn,
  for the spoiler was coming.[115]
Fifth time: Daniel, in captivity, sought God in

sackcloth and ashes.[116]

Sixth time: the king of Nineveh repented in
sackcloth and ashes.[117]

Seventh time: Jesus declared that Tyre and Sidon
would have repented in sackcloth and ashes.[118]

Eighth time: Jesus' words, again, about Tyre
and Sidon.[119]

Eight times: the number of new beginnings.

Repent.

And start again.

Travail

When Esther's eunuchs and maids
Told her about Mordecai's sackcloth and ashes
She was in

Great distress,
Exceeding grief,
Writhing in pain,
Travail.

She didn't yet know the reason
For Mordecai's bitter cry,

But his pain cut her to the quick.

Comfort Sent

Esther sent Mordecai comfortable clothes.
What was she thinking?

Did she think he had been mugged,
And simply needed replacement garments?

Was she embarrassed by the impropriety of his
    extravagant grief,
And wanted to hush him up?

Was she worried about penalties or punishments
For showing public dishevelment?

Or was she already so raw from her life,
That anything she could do to ease another's pain,
    she would do?

Refused

When Mordecai refused to change into Esther's
    offered comfortable clothes,
Esther sent Hathak, a eunuch, to find out the
    reason for his display.

There in the open square of the city, in front of
    the king's gate,
Mordecai told Hathak the whole story,

Down to the detail of Haman's promised price
To destroy the Jews.

Mordecai then gave Hathak a copy of the law of
    annihilation—
Proof that he spoke the truth. No hope that this
    was merely idle gossip.

A Mediated Conversation

Mordecai to Hathak: Show this copy of the law
to Esther and explain it to her. Instruct her to
go into the king's presence to beg for mercy and
plead with him for her people.

Hathak to Esther: Reported what Mordecai said.

Esther to Hathak: Say to Mordecai, "All the
king's officials and the people of the royal
provinces know that for any man or woman who
approaches the king in the inner court without
being summoned the king has but one law: that
they be put to death unless the king extends the
gold scepter to them and spares their lives. But
thirty days have passed since I was called to go
to the king."[120]

Hathak to Mordecai: Reported what Esther said.

Mordecai to Hathak: Take this answer back to
Esther: "Do not think that because you are in
the king's house you alone of all the Jews will
escape. For if you remain silent at this time,
relief and deliverance for the Jews will arise
from another place, but you and your father's
family will perish. And who knows but that you
have come to your royal position for such a time

as this?"[121]

Hathak to Esther: Reported what Mordecai said.

Esther to Hathak: Send this reply to Mordecai:
  "Go, gather together all the Jews who are in
  Susa, and fast for me. Do not eat or drink for
  three days, night or day. I and my attendants
  will fast as you do. When this is done, I will go
  to the king, even though it is against the law.
  And if I perish, I perish."[122]

Hathak to Mordecai: Reported what Esther said.

"So Mordecai went away and carried out all of
  Esther's instructions."[123]

Trusted

In the midst of a court filled with intrigue,
How wonderful to find a trusted go-between,
Fit to entrust personal and dangerous messages.

Just how many machinations did this
    conversation require?

Desperation

Could this very conversation,
Publicly seeking to determine Mordecai's grief,
Be enough connection
To establish Esther's family and cultural
   background,
Despite her years of hiding?

Death Penalty

Enter the king's presence at risk of death—

Unless he extends the golden scepter.
What prompted this extreme rule?

All the normal sources remain silent.
It simply was the law of the land.

Like gravity, it must be obeyed.

But we can surmise:

Protection of the king's time, of his person.
An assassin would think twice before an attempt,
If he knew his own skin was forfeit, even
    before killing.

Maintance of the public order.
If, god-like, the king holds the power of life
    and death,
Who would challenge his rule?
(Not to mention the constant boost to his own
    self-confidence.)

A personal buffer.
As king, what a privilege, to keep complete order
    over your life,

Like the billionaire who would rent the top three
    floors of the hotel:
His staff, his bodyguards, and himself, all removed
    from the rabble.

And so Esther would have to enter,

At odds with
The king's self-protection, his sense of person and
    importance,
And even against the public order.

The Law Made Personal

One thing to have an irrevocable law declaring death
In a year.

Another thing to have an irrevocable law
    declaring death
Immediately.

Not the dread of looming annihilation later,
But the intentional choice to walk into one's probable
    death now.

Made more probable by the king's past issues with
An insubordinate wife.

Made even more probable by the thirty day absence
From his bedchamber.

Out of favor at the moment.
Asked to do a task that would put anyone out of favor:

Go to the king and ask him to overturn
What he established with his best friend and
    drinking buddy.

And Haman was clearly closer to the king's heart
Than was Esther.

Older

Five years into her position as queen,
Esther would still have been young,
But could have borne several children,
The physical perfection of youth
Already faded.

In a court where wine and women flowed freely,
What could keep a king's attention ...

Let alone his affection?

Mordecai's Speech of Persuasion

"Esther, do not imagine,
Take no confidence,
That you will escape
Because you live in the house of the king.

Rather, have confidence that
Deliverance will come to the Jews.
But also have confidence that
If you refuse to act,
You will perish,
Along with your father's family.

Including me.
Remember how you went into travail
Simply because I was wearing
Uncomfortable clothes?
How will you handle your culpability for
  my death?"

Absolute Confidence

Relief and deliverance
Will arise.

No question that this
Impossible situation

Will
Change.

Absolute confidence
In the real beyond the visible.

The faithfulness of God
Will prevail.

The Most Famous Line in this Book

"Who knows but that you have come
To your royal position
For such a time as this?"[124]

You may be afraid, but don't you see?
Perhaps you were made queen
For this very occasion and purpose!

"For Such a Time As This"

Mordecai told Esther,
"You need to go to the king,
Because you ascended specifically for this time,
And you have a unique place to be able to
Intervene in this impending horrific event."

When Mordecai said this,
He announced a
Suddenly.
Life was going along in a particular direction, and then,
Suddenly,
The Lord intervened.

Suddenly Joseph rose from the prison to the palace.
Suddenly Pharaoh released the children of Israel from
    enslavement.

Suddenly, to occupied Palestine,
Jesus came.

Live in hope.
Just because you've been plodding along in a
    particular way
Doesn't mean that you'll do this forever.

Sometimes the
Suddenly comes.

To Gain Courage

Throughout the scriptures,
When in extremity,
And when looking for a shift,
God's people fasted and prayed.

A fast with no food and water, though—
That's not generally recommended.
The kidneys need water to keep working.
And yet—this mandate makes sense
As a desperate attempt to prevent a people's
    destruction.

The Corporate Fast

More than 200 years before,
Jonah went to Nineveh to proclaim,
"Yet forty days, and Nineveh shall be
    overthrown."[125]

The king of Nineveh put on sackcloth and sat
    in the dust,
And called a corporate fast of food and drink for
    the people.
"Who knows? God may yet relent
And with compassion turn from his fierce anger
So that we will not perish."[126]

It worked.
God stayed his hand of judgment.

And if God would respond thus
To a corporate fast by a godless people,
How much more to the apple of his eye?[127]

Dual Actors

Mordecai needed Esther.
Esther needed Mordecai.

Esther had no source of information,
No source of encouragement.

But once commissioned,
She had the next part of the plan.

Fast.
Then go to the king.

Mordecai gave instruction.
Esther gave instruction.

Esther would do what Mordecai said.
Mordecai did what Esther said.

A Reflection on Impossibility

Because we know the end from the beginning,
How easy to read over the sheer
Impossibility
Of the task set before Esther.

The king had trust issues around women.
First wife crossed him, so he banished her.
Esther he could kill simply for dropping by
    uninvited—
A threat she clearly considered possible.

And the king hadn't called for her for thirty days.
She was clearly out of favor at the moment,
Not an intimate and beloved partner.
Someone else was sharing the king's bedchamber.

But even if she happened to survive the initial
    encounter,
What could she say in her few moments of
    attention
To persuade her husband
That his best friend had plotted annihilation?

How to break the king's trust with Haman,
And ally her cause to the king's ...
All while delicately pointing out that, really,
    Ahasuerus, it was your fault.

(Would he, could he, take responsibility?)

Not to mention that the king had shown
Repeated lack of good judgment,
An excessive fondness for wine,
And a quick temper.

And to compound the issue:
This was a law that could not be revoked.
Legally, how could the Jews survive?
Even if the king wanted to repeal the decree ... he
    could not.

And to make matters worse:
The clock was ticking.
The empire extended from India to Ethiopia.
Even should the law be modified ... was there time
    to broadcast the news?

And to make matters even worse:
The law activated an entire people to destruction,
By holding out the promise of material gain.
Turn on your neighbor, and take their stuff!

And worst of all, God had hidden his face,
And promised destruction for disobedience.
No guarantee of help from that direction.
Perhaps this was his plan of judgment all along.

How to Win at War

In the simplest of card games,
The game of War,
Two players lay down cards.
Higher card takes both.

In this game of War,
Haman held
The ace of money,
Which gave him the king.
The queen was in his power.
Mordecai the jack as well.

To round out the numbers,
Haman held the ten, the position of authority as vizier,
The nine, the position of closest friend and confidante,
The eight, the law already in place.

For seven, he literally held the king's ring for
    unlimited power.

For six, he had free access to the palace.
For five, he was a man.
For four, he had the king's trust.

If this was the game of War,
Esther held no cards of significance.

How much could fading looks be worth?
No chance.

SCENE 5

The Third Day

In the scriptures, the number three denotes
   completeness,
Divine perfection.
In the creation story, the first three days complete
   the fundamentals:

Day One: let there be light.
Day Two: let there be waters above and
   waters beneath.
Day Three: let there be land, and let there be
   growing things.

The next three days decorate the fundamentals:

Day Four: let there be sun, moon, and stars.
Day Five: let there be birds and fish.
Day Six: let there be land animals and man.

The number three also denotes *resurrection*,

As on Day Three, the land rose up from
   the waters,
And the growing things rose up from the earth.
A small foreshadowing of another resurrection on
   the third day.

New Life for Israel

On the third day,
Esther put on her royal robes.

It was time for a new life for Israel,
For that which was dead to be given life again.

She stood in the inner court, in front of the
    king's hall.
From his royal throne, the king saw her.

She obtained favor in his sight. Again.

As at their first meeting:
Grace, charm, elegance, acceptance.

Well-favored. Pleasant, precious, gracious.
Subjective kindness, objective beauty.

Because of Esther's beauty and grace,
Other people were beautiful and graceful toward her.

The king held out to her the golden scepter that was
    in his hand,
Extending permission, acceptance.
So Esther drew near and touched the tip of
    the scepter.
Favor instead of death.

The Request Made at the Risk of a Life

The king asked,
"What is it, Queen Esther? What is your request?
Even up to half the kingdom, it will be
    given you."[128]

Presumably the king knew the punishment for
    appearing unexpectedly.
The stakes were high enough,
Esther didn't show up just on a whim. She needed
    something.

The true request, of course, was for the repeal of
    the unrepealable law.
But how to first unravel the
    attachment to Haman?
What kind of impossible assignment, in the midst
    of a crazy court?

Savvy marketers know about pre-framing:
When a person agrees to a small request,
This increases the likelihood of agreeing to a
    larger request later.

Esther made a small request.

Banquet

"If it pleases the king,
Let the king and Haman
Come this day
To a banquet
I have prepared for him."

"What Is That in Your Hand?"

God spoke to Moses out of the burning bush.
Moses was manifestly unexcited by God's call
    on his life.
He had all manner of questions and excuses.

When Moses asked,
"What if they do not believe me or listen to
    me and say,
'The Lord did not appear to you'?"

The Lord said to him,
"What is that in your hand?"[129]
And then developed a strategy using the staff
    in his hand.

Moses was not empty-handed.

What did Esther have?
She knew the king loved wine.
And so she invited the king and Haman to,
    literally, a drinking party.[130]

God Still at Work,
Behind the Scenes

When Esther said,
"Let the king and Haman come this day,"

The initial letters of these words in Hebrew
Form an acrostic,
Spelling out the name of God.

YHVH.

As if, in order to express "LORD,"
The author wrote:
"Let Our Royal Dinner
This day be graced by the king and Haman."[131]

Esther the Jewish queen spoke.

Initial letters initiated God's action,
And the words formed God's name
   spelled forward.
God rules and Esther acted,
Moving forward to a great end.

Invitation Accepted

The king accepted, even telling
Haman to make haste,
That he may do what Esther had said.

So the king and Haman went to the banquet
   Esther had prepared.

The Rules of Hospitality

Today we enjoy hospitality
As a time of food and fellowship.

But in other times, in other cultures,
Hospitality meant a strengthening of
    relational bonds.

No prior record of any intimate dinner parties
Between this husband and wife.

A demonstration of a slight shift
In relational connection.

Not such a frivolous invitation
As it might appear.

Diplomacy

Daniel, in the court of Babylon, refused the
  king's wine.
Esther, in the court of Persia, drank wine
  with the king.

"As they were drinking wine, the king again
  asked Esther,
'Now what is your petition?
It will be given you.
And what is your request?
Even up to half the kingdom, it will be
  granted.'"[132]

Both Daniel and Esther served God's purposes
In their respective places. But through very
  different means.

Let the Lord guide you.
Let him guide others, too.

The Second Request Made at the Risk of a Life

Esther replied, "My petition and my request
   is this...."

And we all lean in to hear
How she will address this tricky subject.

But instead of addressing it, she punted.

"If the king regards me with favor"—
That beautiful word *favor* again,
Grace, charm, elegance, acceptance—

"And if it pleases the king to grant my petition
   and fulfill my request,
Let the king and Haman come
Tomorrow
To the banquet I will prepare for them.
Then I will answer the king's question."[133]

Did she betray just a hint of nervousness here?
"Petition" and "request," though different words
   in Hebrew,
Both mean "petition" and "request," almost a
   direct overlay.

What happened at that banquet to make
   her delay?
Too much wine flowing too early?
Haman too loquacious? The king too distracted?
Did she end the evening with a sense of failure?

Or was this always her plan,
To see how much favor she had before she
   made her move?

For all the fasting, she hadn't made much
   progress yet.
Merely acknowledged that she had a request.

What check in her spirit did she sense, to keep
   her quiet,
And try the patience of the king yet once more?

Happiness

"Haman went out that day
Happy and in
High spirits."[134]

The word "happy,"
Also translated:

Rejoice.
Glad.
Joyful.
Merry.
Merrily.
Merryhearted.

Blithe or gleeful.

As in: "Let the heavens be *glad*,
Let the earth rejoice:
And let them say among the nations,
'The LORD reigns!'"[135]

The phrase "high spirits,"
Could also be "glad heart."

Haman had a good inner man,
A good seat of emotions.

The word "good"
Means "good" in the widest possible sense.
Good as an adjective descriptor,
Good as a stand-alone noun.

Think: "And God saw the light,
That it was *good*.[136]

Part of the reason we should enjoy
Happy emotions, but not trust them:

Because the only one in the story who feels thus
Was Haman, who was working against God's plan.

Unchanged

Directly from the delight of Esther's first feast,
Haman encountered Mordecai at the king's gate.

Mordecai did not rise, nor stir—
His pattern of life unchanged by the coming
    retributive disaster.

Haman was filled with rage against Mordecai.
In the Hebrew, literally: "Haman was being filled
    on Mordecai fury."

All Haman's euphoria vanished in an instant.
No pleasant evening of drink and
    selective company

Could wipe away the torment of Mordecai's
    refusal to comply.
This interaction's emotional sting remained
    unchanged.

Pause for a Moment

Mordecai, responsible now
For the lives of all the Jews in Persia,
Had to consciously make the decision
Again
Not to prostrate himself.

Evil had, for all appearances,
Triumphed.

Doomed by decree.

He could grovel now ...
It probably wouldn't make a difference.
But who knows?
It might!

When a bully turns to attack,
Some cower; some stay strong.

After a bully attacks,
How painful to continue to deliberately defy.

How terrible the invitation:
Stay the course.

An Insufferable Man

At the gate of the king,
Haman held himself back, restrained himself,
Did nothing to Mordecai,
And went home.

"Calling together his friends and Zeresh, his wife,
Haman boasted to them about his vast wealth,
His many sons,
And all the ways the king had honored him
And how he had elevated him
Above the other nobles and officials.

'And that's not all,' Haman added.
'I'm the only person Queen Esther invited
To accompany the king
To the banquet she gave.
And she has invited me along with the king tomorrow.'"[137]

Presumably this was not the only time
He ever called people together
To hear him brag.

How much could the friends actually like this
    insufferable man?
The parties and the wealth—sure.
But the man himself?
How many friends could he have had?

And after all this boasting,
He ended on a whine about the one person who
   defied him:

"But all this gives me no satisfaction
As long as I see that Jew Mordecai sitting at the
   king's gate."[138]

God Still at Work, Even in the House of an Enemy

When Haman said,
"But all this gives me no satisfaction,"

The final letters of these words in Hebrew
Form an acrostic,
Spelling out the name of God.

But in reverse.

Not YHVH,
But HVHY,

As if, in order to express "LORD,"
The author wrote:
"Yet am I
saD; foR, nO avaiL
Is all this to me."[139]

Haman the Gentile spoke.

Final letters demonstrated that the end was
    coming even now.
And the words formed God's name backwards,
For God was overruling Haman's glee,
And turning back his evil counsels.
Haman's end was coming.

A Brilliant Plan

Haman's wife Zeresh and all his friends advised:

"Set up an extravagant pole,
Seventy-five feet high,[140]
And in the morning ask the king
To let Mordecai hang on it.

After Mordecai's demise,
Then go to the banquet tomorrow
And be happy again."

This suggestion pleased Haman.

It set him to rights,
Restored him,
Made him whole.

And he had the pole set up.

PART TWO
COMEDY

SCENE 6

The Reversal Begins

"That night the king could not sleep."[141]
The literal Hebrew: "The sleep of the king
  flitted away."

On such a slender thread hung
The fate of a people.

The Sleep of the King Flitted Away

The straight read might be that the king,
Energized and excited by his time with the queen,
Couldn't sleep.

Perhaps. But a copious quantity of wine
Usually acts as a soporific,
Not a stimulant.

Perhaps the king slept, but then woke from a
  nightmare,
In which Bigthan and Teresh are coming
  after him.
The question comes to mind: Who to trust?[142]

The Put-Me-to-Sleep Solution

Today many people read to fall asleep.
Apparently this has been true for
    thousands of years.

The king ordered the book of the record of his
    reign to be read.
Perhaps the list of names would be a
    good sedative.

Hidden in Plain Sight

"For there is nothing hidden that will not be
   disclosed,
And nothing concealed that will not be known or
   brought out into the open."[143]

As the king listened, he heard the name Mordecai:
How he had uncovered the assassination plot of
   Bigthan and Teresh,

Now a half decade or more ago.

Shouldn't an assassination attempt be more
   memorable?

But ancient kings required cupbearers to ensure
   their wine was not poisoned.
Perhaps death threats were so routine, another
   assassination attempt was easy to forget.

Or perhaps the king mentioned the plot to his
   secret service,
And they carried out the dirty work, so that it
   filled his mind only a few minutes.

And would he have been partially inebriated at
   the time anyway?

Expansive

In the open and generous frame of mind
From a pleasant time with his queen,
The king wondered:

"How did we honor and esteem Mordecai?
Did we recognize him, or proclaim his greatness?"

The first time he's shown to think
Of someone else's honor and greatness.

Evidence of God already at work.

Thus far, only the king has been shown any honor.
But now ... a shift.

"The king's heart is like a stream of water directed
    by the LORD;
He guides it wherever he pleases."[144]

Soon Remedied

The attendants answered as expected: "Nothing has been done for him."[145]

Thus far, nothing ...

But the change was coming.

Dispatch

The king, showing all his typical impetuosity,
Determined not to wait to celebrate.

Sure, it was, at best, barely day,
But why not see who might be around to advise?

Arrival

Haman, that other impetuous character,
Acting on the advice of his wife,
Had arrived at the court.

She had said to go to the king,
"In the morning,"
And surely early morning counts.

Expectation

Haman had come to court
To ask to suspend Mordecai on the pole.

Since the king had shown extreme indifference
To wiping out an entire people,

Haman had every right to expect that the
  smaller request

Of a single man's death would be

Favorably granted.

Audible Dialogue

King to attendants: Who is in the court?

Attendants to king: Haman is standing in
the court.

King to attendants: Bring him in.

King to Haman: What should be done for the man
the king delights to honor?[146]

Inner Monologue

Since the previous morning,
Haman had been singled out for an exclusive feast
  with the queen,
Then spent time with his friends, recounting his
  successes.
He was basking in the reality of the approaching
  annihilation of the Jews,
And eagerly anticipating no difficulty to kill his
  archenemy Mordecai.

From this self-satisfied—but understandable and
  relatable—perspective,
Haman said in his heart:

"Who is there that the king would rather honor
  than me?"[147]

Pause for a Moment

Think about the preciousness of the
    king's question.
For the man whose life was shown honor at all
    time (excepting Vashti),
He didn't know how to honor another.

For him, his entire position gives him nothing
    but honor.
He genuinely doesn't know what honor looks like,
Nor how to show it to someone else.

"What should be done for the man the king
    delights to honor?"[148]

This question has no easy answer.

The king was not asking about repayment
    or reward.
That would be easy enough:
Some land, some money.

Rather, the question: I hold a person in
    high esteem.
How can I demonstrate that?

Haman Reveals How He Would Like to Be Honored

"For the man the king delights to honor,
Have them bring a royal robe the king has worn
And a horse the king has ridden,
One with a royal crest placed on its head.
Then let the robe and horse be entrusted to one of
   the king's most noble princes.
Let them robe the man the king delights to honor,
And lead him on the horse through the
   city streets,
Proclaiming before him,
'This is what is done for the man the king delights
   to honor!'"[149]

Dispatch II

The king, showing all his typical impetuosity,
Determined not to wait to venerate.

Sure, it was, at best, barely day,
But no time like the present!

"Go at once and do all you have suggested
For Mordecai the Jew, who sits at the king's gate."

The Turn of the Screw

"Who sits at the king's gate."

The profane king, seeking to be helpful,
Clarified for Haman which Mordecai.
Not the fruit-seller or fish-monger, but the one
    who sits at the king's gate.

What is Mordecai's defining, outstanding feature?
When all others prostrated themselves before
    the evil man,
Mordecai sat.

Or maybe stood.

He did not fall face down to honor what should
    not be honored.
The king and the King say:
"Honor Mordecai the Jew. He sits at the
    king's gate."

Rise on the Horizon

Mordecai, sitting at the gate, prompted the ruling
That all Jews be killed.

Mordecai, still sitting at the gate,
Now saw the beginning of the great reversal.

As he sat in proxy for the people,
His rise, and theirs, was coming.

Overturned Expectations

Haman had hoped to be able to go with guards
And summon Mordecai with glee
And bring him to his home
And display his corpse on a pole
In shame.

Instead

Haman, as a noble prince, had to go
And summon Mordecai with mortification
And bring him through the streets
And display him on the king's horse
In honor.

Through Every Street

The point of public execution
Was public spectacle.

Train the city's inhabitants in behavioral
    expectations:
What was good, and what was bad.

Haman had expected that through every street
    would resound the cry,
"This is what is done for the man the king delights
    to destroy!"

Rather, he himself spread the cry:
"This is what is done for the man the king delights
    to honor!"

On Such a Slender Thread

Note that, in the larger story,
Not much has changed yet:

Haman, still second in command.
The Jews, still sentenced to death.

In light of the overwhelming impending
    catastrophe,
How much hope could Mordecai's day of
    honor bring?

And yet: Elijah's servant saw the rain coming from
"A cloud as small as a man's hand."

When God acts, sometimes the action
Starts small.

Aftermath

After all his honor,
Mordecai returned to the king's gate.

After all his dishonor,
Haman hurried home, his head covered in grief.

He told his wife Zeresh and all his friends
Everything that had happened to him.

Yesterday the wife and friends recommended
    Mordecai's immediate demise.
Today they realized the truth:

"If Mordecai, who has started your downfall,
Is of the seed of the Jews,

You cannot stand against him—
You will surely fall before him."

Summoned

"While they were still talking with him,
The king's eunuchs arrived
And hurried Haman away
To the banquet Esther had prepared."[150]

Haman now hadn't slept
For the last day and a half.

He had spent his day like a servant,
Walking the dusty streets, shouting
To honor the man in all the world
He most despised.

He had suffered the shock
Of a great reversal.

His wife and closest friends,
Rather than encouraging him,
Now predicted his imminent demise,
As he was opposing the Jews.

Just how tired were his feet?
And had he even bathed?

Where one day he went in pride
And eager anticipation,
Today, disheveled and filled with dread,
He must have gone reluctantly ... at best.

SCENE 7

The Second Banquet

"So the king and Haman went
To Queen Esther's banquet."[151]

In the Hebrew: "The king and Haman
Were coming to drink with Esther the queen."

Very appropriate description
For this king's court.

The king, enthusiastic and oblivious.
Haman, simmering, fearful, and furious.

Over Wine

As they were drinking wine,
The king again asked,

"Queen Esther, what is your petition?
It will be given you.
What is your request?
Even up to half the kingdom, it will be granted."

And now the fullness of time had come.
Any earlier, and the reversal had not yet found its
    full effect.
Any later and the moment would have passed.

Nothing for it now but to speak.

Queen Esther's Petition

"If I have found favor with you, Your Majesty,
And if it pleases you, grant me my life—
This is my petition.
And spare my people—
This is my request.

For I and my people have been sold to be

Destroyed,
Killed
And annihilated.

If we had merely been sold as male and
    female slaves,
I would have kept quiet,
Because no such distress would justify disturbing
    the king."[152]

Petition, Expanded

Esther rhetorically wonders
If she had found favor with the king.
Was the king determined to be
Graceful and beautiful to her?

If so:
My life.
That's my petition.

And my people, too.
That's my request.

My people and I have been sold to be

Exterminated.
Killed.
Destroyed.

Yes, I can quote the exact words of the edict.

Sold to be annihilated.

If we'd been simply sold as slaves,
That would have not been worth mentioning.

Sold

An interesting thread of economics runs through
the book of Esther.
Haman, with his offer of ten thousand talents
of silver.

Esther claimed that they have been sold ...
Apparently the payment actually went through.

And how to entice people to rise up against their
neighbors?
Offer the promise of their goods as bounty!

And though in one possible translation Esther says
that she would have kept quiet
If she had only been sold, and not sold to
the death,

"Because no such distress would justify disturbing
the king,"[153]
Alternately, this passage could read,

"But the compensation our adversary offers
Cannot be compared with the loss the king
would suffer."[154]

Another read: "The enemy could not
Countervail the king's damage."[155]

Countervail: "to offset the effect of something,
By countering it with something of equal force."[156]

Ten thousand talents, eleven million ounces
   of silver
Would not be enough to offset the damage
   to the king.

The Jews, as God's chosen people, bring
   prosperity.
Annihilate them for (possible) short term gain,
   but long term

Loss.

God at Work in the House of the King

King Ahasuerus asked Queen Esther,
"Who is he, and where is he—
The man who has dared to do such a thing?"

When the king said,
"Who is he, and where is he?"

The final letters of these words in Hebrew
Form an acrostic,
Spelling out the name of God
Given to Moses,

But in reverse.

Not EHYH, "I Am,"
But HYHE.

As if, in order to write the acronym EHYH,
The author wrote:
"Who was it who
presumetH alwaY finishetH herE?"

"This is my name forever,
The name you shall call me
From generation to generation."[157]

Who is he and where is he?
What agency pushed forward this wicked plan?

Not just human agency.

Who will deliver from Haman?
The same who delivered from Pharaoh in the
  day of Moses.

God's Name

Moses asked God about his name.
"When the children of Israel ask who sent me,
What name shall I give them?"

God said to Moses, "I am who I am.
This is what you are to say to the Israelites:
'I am has sent me to you.'"[158]

An alternative translation is:
"I will be what I will be,
And I will write the story I will write."[159]

Here, God writes a powerful story.

Named

Esther finally spoke the name:
"'An adversary and enemy! This vile Haman!'
Then Haman was terrified before the king
    and queen."[160]

Think what a reversal:
One day before the accusation would have felt
    ridiculous.
Today, completely believable.

The king and queen, presenting a united front.

Clear Vision

"The king got up in a rage,
Left his wine
And went out into the palace garden."[161]

A moment of truth for him:
Leave the mind-numbing alcohol
In exchange for insight.

Leave behind the fogginess of mind.

"But Haman, realizing
That the king had already decided his fate,
Stayed behind to beg Queen Esther for his life."

Put another way: "Haman stood up
To make request for his life to Esther the queen;
For he saw that there was evil determined against
    him by the king."[162]

God at Work in the House of the King

When the narrator said,
"That there was evil determined against him,"

The final letters of these words in Hebrew
Form an acrostic,
Spelling out the name of God.

YHVH.

As if, in order to express "LORD,"
The author wrote:
"For he saw that there was
eviL tO feaR determineD
Against him by the king."[163]

Final letters show Haman's end had come
And the words form God's name forward,
For God rules and brings about the end he seeks.
The end had come.

One Final Power Play

In modern Western societies, men and women
   touch in various ways:
Handshakes.
A pat on the shoulder or arm.
Brief hugs among friends.

This was not normal in ancient times,
When men and women were kept firmly apart.
The women in the king's household saw only
Eunuchs, and the king.
And, for two banquets, Haman.

"Just as the king returned
From the palace garden to the banquet hall,
Haman was falling on the couch
Where Esther was reclining.
The king exclaimed, 'Will he even molest
   the queen
While she is with me in the house?'"[164]

In what context did Haman think falling on a
   reclining female
Would be appropriate?

The text is unclear:
Was he trying an intense form of intimidation?
Did he lose his balance, after a day in the sun?

The text does not claim that he sought to ravish
  the queen.
But so it appeared to the furious king.

Of course, Haman did seek to "molest,"
As in "persecute,"
Not only the queen, but all her people.

So whatever the king may have thought he saw in
  the natural,

The underlying truth was darker, was death.

Witnesses

"As soon as the word left the king's mouth,
They covered Haman's face."[165]

An odd detail: were the eunuchs and attendants
Standing around as this intense scene transpire?

Or did the king's shout summon the attendants,
Waiting outside the door?

In any case, Harbona, one of the king's attendants,
Offered a ready solution:
"A 75 foot pole stands by Haman's house.
He set it up for Mordecai, who spoke up to help
   the king."

And so here we find another unexpected witness,
   finally finding a voice.
First Esther, then the king's own eyes, and now
   Harbona the eunuch.

God's word, in the law of Moses:
"One witness is not enough to convict
   anyone accused
Of any crime or offense they may have committed.
A matter must be established by the testimony of
   two or three witnesses."[166]

All three gave testimony.

Capital Punishment

The king said, "Hang Haman on his pole!"

So they suspended Haman
On the pole he had prepared for Mordecai.

Then the king's fury subsided.

SCENE 8

Setting to Rights

That same day King Ahasuerus
Gave Queen Esther the estate of Haman,
The enemy of the Jews.

And since Haman had offered the king
Twelve million ounces of silver,
Presumably this was not a petty acquisition.

The Big Reveal

Esther, no longer in secret,
Had made known her nationality,
And now also revealed her family background.

Cousin Mordecai ... now that name meant
    something.

And Mordecai, no longer sitting,
Came into the presence of the king.

Entrusted

"The king took off his signet ring,
Which he had reclaimed from Haman,
And presented it to Mordecai.
And Esther appointed him over
  Haman's estate."[167]

Mordecai, having proven his trustworthiness,
Advanced almost instantly.
Now he stepped into a new role:
Steward of a large estate.

But Setting All to Rights Takes Time

Just because the enemy is dead
Does not mean that all his plans have also been
  overturned.

There remained much work to be done.

The plot to annihilate the Jews, conceived and
  implemented,
Remained in place.

Esther must take courage in hand again.

Return to the King's Presence

"Esther again pleaded with the king,
Falling at his feet and weeping.
She begged him to put an end to the evil plan of
    Haman the Agagite,
Which he had devised against the Jews.

Then the king extended the gold scepter to Esther
And she arose and stood before him.

'If it pleases the king,' she said,
'And if he regards me with favor
And thinks it the right thing to do,
And if he is pleased with me,

Let an order be written overruling
The dispatches that Haman son of Hammedatha,
    the Agagite,
Devised and wrote to destroy the Jews in all the
    king's provinces.
For how can I bear to see disaster fall on
    my people?
How can I bear to see the destruction of my
    family?'"[168]

The Plan and the Action

The three—Mordecai, Esther, and Ahasuerus—
Together could figure out how to roll back an
   evil plan.

King Ahasuerus said to Queen Esther and to
   Mordecai the Jew:
"I gave Haman's house to Esther,
And they hung him on the pole he set up,
Because he sought to lay hands on the Jews.

Now write to the Jews, as it seems good to you,
In the name of the king,
And sealed with the king's ring—
For no document written in the king's name,
And sealed with his ring, can be repealed."

At once the king's scribes were called.

Déjà Vu

On the twenty-third day of the third month, the
    month of Sivan,[169]
The royal secretaries were summoned.

In the language and script of each province
    and people—
And also to the Jews in their script and language.

They wrote all Mordecai's orders
To the king's lieutenants, governors, and nobles
In all of the 127 provinces, from India to Ethiopia.

In the name of King Ahasuerus was it written,
And sealed with the king's ring,
And sent by swift riders to all the king's
    provinces.

"To the Jews: you have the right to assemble
    and defend,
And the right to

Exterminate.
Kill.
Destroy.

On the thirteenth day of the twelfth month,
Should anyone come with intent to harm

Your women and children.

And should they attack,
Once they're gone, plan to loot and
Plunder their goods."

A copy of the writing of the law
Went to every province and was made known to
   the people of every nationality
So the Jews would be ready for that day,
To avenge themselves on their enemies.

Spurred by the king's word,
The couriers went out, swiftly riding the royal
   horses, carrying
This law of the Persians and Medes that cannot
   be repealed.

And the edict was given at Susa the palace.

Speed

Earlier, when Haman's declaration went forth,
Runners carried the word to the farthest reaches
   of the king's empire.

One piece of the impossible puzzle:
Even if the king somehow reversed his decree,

How would the news reach the people in time?
Rather than runners, this announcement went out

Via couriers, swiftly riding the royal horses.

There is always a solution.

Salvation Expansion

Earlier, Mordecai and Esther
Teamed together to save the king.

Now Mordecai and Esther
Teamed together to save the people.

Decoration

When the king held the feast that brought
   Vashti's downfall,

The decorations of the palace were pale cotton
   and amethyst,
With lines of fine linen and purple,
Held up by silver rings on marble pillars.

Now Mordecai went out, clothed in pale cotton
   and amethyst,
With a garment of fine linen and purple.

But he had a great crown—a large ring, if you
   will—of gold, not silver,
Showing that a superior pillar had come,

Showing that Mordecai was the true splendor and
   support of the palace.

Mordecai's Ascension

When Mordecai left the king's presence,
Wearing his royal garments,

"The city of Susa held a joyous celebration.

For the Jews it was a time of
Happiness and joy,
Gladness and honor.

In every province
And in every city
To which the edict of the king came,
There was joy and gladness among the Jews,
With feasting and celebrating.

And many people of other nationalities
Became Jews
Because fear of the Jews had seized them."[170]

Celebration

"For the Jews it was a time of happiness and joy,
    gladness and honor."[171]

At the start of this story, the city of Susa
    had a feast.

A feast should be a celebration,
And yet the first party crackled with tension
And drunkenness.

Here, now, the city of Susa rejoiced and was glad
In their joyous celebration.

Happiness.
Joy.
Gladness.
Honor.

Light.
Gladness.
Joy.
Honor.

Light.
Rejoicing.
Elation.
Esteem.[172]

Outward

At the start of the story,
Ahasuerus summoned people to the capital
For an extended feast.

Now, as the edict went out,
In every city, the Jews had joy and gladness,
Feasting and celebrating.

Rather than the party coming in,
This party went out.

Fear

What is this "fear" that fell upon all people?

The Old Testament uses several words for "fear."

"The fear of the LORD is the beginning of
    knowledge,
But fools despise wisdom and instruction,"[173]
In this case, "The fear of the LORD"
"Also implies submission, awe, worship, and
    reverence."[174]

The fear that fell was not this kind of fear.

Here, when the passage reads "fear of the Jews had
    seized them,"[175]
What fell on the people was a different word, like
    what Job proclaimed:
"What I feared has come upon me; what I dreaded
    has happened to me."[176]

The people felt fear, terror, dread toward the Jews.

What a gift.

Fear and terror would be powerful deterrents to
    casual attack.
How much less likely to attempt to annihilate.

Blessed

God's promise to Abraham:
"I will bless those who bless you,
And whoever curses you I will curse;
And all peoples on earth will be blessed
    through you."[177]

As the people throughout the Persian empire
Observed the great reversal that the Lord
    brought about,

Many of the people of the land,
Rather than looking forward to killing the Jews,
Became practicing Jews,
For the fear of the Jews—
And, unstated but still true, the fear of the
    Jews' God—
Fell upon them.

Blessings for those who bless:
Fulfilled—
At least in part.

SCENE 9

The Thirteenth Day Came

When the thirteenth day of the twelfth
    month arrived,
The day the enemies of the Jews had hoped to
    overpower them,
Instead the Jews had the power over those who
    hated them.

The Jews assembled in their cities in all the
    provinces,
Ready to lay hands on any who would seek
    their hurt,
But none could withstand them. And the fear of
    them fell on all the people.

And the nobles, lieutenants, governors,
And the king's administrators
Helped the Jews,
Because the fear of Mordecai had fallen
    upon them.

Fear of Mordecai

The people in the provinces feared the Jews,
But the fear of Mordecai also fell on the rulers,

"For Mordecai was great in the king's house,
And his fame went out throughout all the
    provinces:
For this man Mordecai waxed greater and
    greater."[178]

When the scripture uses the Hebrew word "ish"
    for "male" or "man,"
This word emphasizes a great man in contrast
    with ordinary men.
Here is Mordecai: great in the house, famous in
    the provinces,

A great man who grew greater and greater.

Smiting

"Thus the Jews smote all their enemies

With the stroke of the sword,
And slaughter,
And destruction,
And did what they would unto those that
     hated them.

And in Shushan the palace
The Jews slew and destroyed five hundred men."[179]

Finished

And Parshandatha,
And Dalphon,
And Aspatha,
And Poratha,
And Adalia,
And Aridatha,
And Parmashta,
And Arisai,
And Aridai,
And Vaizatha,

The ten sons of Haman,
Son of Hammedatha,
The enemy of the Jews,

They killed.

And so Mordecai the Benjamite,
Descended from King Saul's father,
Finished the work entrusted to Saul.

Careful

In the time of the kings, the prophet Samuel told
    the people:
"Now go, attack the Amalekites
And totally destroy all that belongs to them.
Do not spare them; put to death men and women,
    children and infants,
Cattle and sheep, camels and donkeys."[180]

But when Samuel came again, later, and found the
    finest cattle yet alive,
He asked, "Why did you not obey the Lord?
Why did you pounce on the plunder and do evil in
    the eyes of the Lord?"[181]

By the time of King Ahasuerus,
Having faced sure death but come out alive,
The children of Israel had learned their lesson.

Despite explicit permission in the king's law,
"They did not lay their hands on the plunder."[182]

To obey is better than sacrifice.[183]

The Evening of the Thirteenth

After the number of those killed in Susa was
    reported to the king
That same day ...
Note the evidence of greater intimacy:

The king said to Queen Esther,
"The Jews have killed and destroyed five
    hundred men
And the ten sons of Haman
In the citadel of Susa.
What have they done in the rest of the king's
    provinces?

Now what is your petition?
It will be given you.
What is your request?
It will also be granted."[184]

Note the change:
No fear of death to have this conversation.
As the king relaxed into greater trust,
    greater rapport,
He offered news to,
And sought advice from,

His wife.

Esther's Recommendations

Two suggestions,
If it please the king.

First: let the edict extend one more day.
Second: let Haman's dead sons be
    displayed on poles.

Unpleasant Optics

The king issued a law: same rules apply tomorrow.
And Haman's ten sons were hung up for display.

For the former, this request makes sense:
With emotions running high, and the innate
    reflex for revenge,

It's not unreasonable to expect
Persians might want to continue to try to
    massacre.

Let the Jews be ready
To defend with impunity.

But the latter: how unrecognizable, even
    bloodthirsty.
Beautiful Esther seems suddenly akin to Salome,

Asking for the head of John the Baptist on
    a platter.

The cultural divide is wide.

And yet ... savvy generals know
That you don't just fight the battle in front of you,

But the next one, too.

You don't drop the atom bomb for the almost-
   defeated Japanese.
You drop the atom bomb to put Russia on notice.

To those five hundred families in the city of Susa:
Think twice before you rise up in revenge.

Haman was the favorite of the king,
But great was the fall of him,

And of his house,
And of his generations.

Utterly destroyed.
Take note.

Are the aesthetics distasteful?
Yes, of course.

But as an act of mercy,
These optics save lives.

The ten sons of Haman were already dead.
To display them as deterrent against future
   destruction?

A grace for the Jews.
Yes, to prevent more bloodshed.

A grace for the Persians.
Yes, to cool the desire for revenge.

The Fourteenth Day

Esther proved her prudence
As the Jews in Susa again gathered the next day,
And slew another three hundred men.

But even now, they did not lay their hands on
   the plunder.

Total Body Count

As the reports arrived: in the king's provinces,
The Jews assembled together to protect
    themselves,
And seventy-five thousand foes lost their lives.

Such relief from their enemies ...

For if a man would rise up to kill,
He would not have hesitated
To mock, cheat, torment, and pester.

Instead: relief on every side from enemies.

Though Haman may have enticed destruction
With financial gain for the Persians,
Three times over the text makes clear:

The Jews did not lay a hand on the plunder.

Throughout all the provinces,
The Persian deaths were not financially driven,
But simply the Jews lawful right to self-defense.

The Rollback of the Impossible on a Large Scale

In Esther, yes, the impossible reversal
In her generation.
And yet ... far more.

The Jews did not take the offered plunder.
The descendant of Saul's father
Killed the Amalekites.

Here, the opportunity to right a wrong
From many generations before.
Another, greater, rolling back of the previous evil.

Feasting and Authority

Throughout the provinces,
The main fighting happened on the thirteenth,
And on the fourteenth, the Jews rested
And made it a day of feasting and gladness.

"That is why rural Jews—those living in villages—
Observe the fourteenth of the month of Adar
As a day of joy and feasting,
A day for giving presents to each other."[185]

But in the capital Susa,
The Jews assembled on both the thirteenth and
    the fourteenth,
And on the fifteenth, the Jews rested
And made it a day of feasting and gladness.

Authority

In the capital,
The fighting lasted twice as long.

If you live in the place of authority,
Be prepared for a longer battle.

If you choose to be the head,
Assume responsibility, as long as needed.

The Record of Events

Mordecai recorded these events.[186]

He also wrote to all the Jews
Throughout the provinces of King Ahaseurus,
Near and far,
To celebrate annually
The fourteenth and fifteenth days of the
    month of Adar
As the time when the Jews rested, settled down,
    from their enemies,

And as the month when
Their sorrow was turned into joy
And their mourning into a good day.

A "good" day like when God saw that the light
    was "good."

Mordecai wrote the Jews to observe the days
As days of feasting and joy
And giving presents of food to one another
And gifts to the poor.

Purim

"So the Jews agreed to continue the celebration
    they had begun,
Doing what Mordecai had written to them.

For Haman son of Hammedatha, the Agagite,
The enemy of all the Jews,
Had plotted against the Jews to destroy them
And had cast the *pur* (that is, the lot)
For their ruin and destruction.

But when Esther came before the king,
He issued written orders
That the evil scheme Haman had devised
    against the Jews
Should come back onto his own head,
And that he and his sons should be impaled
    on poles.

(Therefore these days were called Purim, from the
    word *pur*.)

Because of everything written in this letter
And because of what they had seen and what had
    happened to them,
The Jews took it on themselves to establish
    the custom
That they and their descendants and all who

join them
Should without fail observe these two days
   every year,
In the way prescribed and at the time appointed.
These days should be remembered and observed
In every generation by every family,
And in every province and in every city.
And these days of Purim should never fail to be
   celebrated by the Jews—
Nor should the memory of these days die out
   among their descendants."[187]

A Little More Paperwork

So Esther the queen, daughter of Abihail,
Along with Mordecai the Jew,
Wrote with all authority
To confirm this second letter of Purim.

And Mordecai sent letters to all the Jews
In the 127 provinces of Ahasuerus' kingdom—
Words of goodwill and assurance, of peace
    and truth—
To confirm these days of Purim at their
    appointed times,
As Mordecai the Jew and Esther the queen had
    decreed for them.

And as they had established for themselves
And their descendants in regard to their times of
    fasting and lamentation.

Esther's decree confirmed these regulations
    about Purim,
And it was written in the records.[188]

Why "Purim"?

Certain names of celebrations make sense:
Passover, because the angel of death passed over
    the firstborns.
The Feast of First Fruits, when the Israelites
    brought their first fruits.

But to name a festival "toss of dice"?
To emphasize not the big-picture triumph
    or reversal,
But the tiny detail of supposed randomness?

But, of course, no randomness.
"The lot is cast into the lap,
But its every decision is from the LORD."[189]

In a story where God was at work, but hidden,
Where the auspicious day turned out to be
    decidedly inauspicious,
Perhaps the very cheekiness of the name
    demonstrates its appropriateness.

SCENE 10

To Conclude

"Ahasuerus laid a tribute on the land, and the
coastlands of the sea."

Why this random detail included
In such a tightly organized and brilliantly
structured story?

It demonstrates in a few words this king's
growing maturity.
The book opens with a party for everyone:
Spend money! Have fun!

It closes with a sign of ruling, which costs money.
Ahasuerus was growing up.

A Matter of Public Record

"And all his acts of power and might,
Together with a full account of the greatness of
Mordecai,
Whom the king had promoted,
Are they not written in the book
Of the annals of the kings of Media
and Persia?"[190]

Two Stars

"It is too small a thing for you to be my servant
To restore the tribes of Jacob
And bring back those of Israel I have kept.

I will also make you a light for the Gentiles,
That my salvation may reach to the ends of
    the earth."[191]

Esther means "star."
Mordecai, too, now a light for the Gentiles.

To Close

Mordecai the Jew was second in rank to King
  Ahasuerus.

He was famous,
Preeminent,
Very great,

Among the Jews,

And held in high esteem,
Accepted,
Well received,
Highly favored,
Highly popular,

By his many kinsmen,
The multitude of his brothers,
His many fellow Jews,

Because he worked for the good,
He sought the welfare,
He continued to pursue prosperity,
Seeking the wealth

Of and for his people,

And spoke for the welfare and peace,

For the well-being,

Of all his countrymen,
The Jews,
His people,
His entire nation,

To all their descendants,

All his seed.[192]

EPILOGUE

One refused to bow.
The net to bring about his destruction
   cinched tight.
Impossible to reverse.

Another partnered with him,
Used the only thing in her hand—
Her disinterested husband's interest in wine.

A sleepless night;
A dramatic reversal.
The unassailable net dissolved.

A people saved.
Long-past wrongs, now righted.
An entire empire blessed.

Refuse to bow.

NOTES

1 An acrostic takes letters from different words or lines of verse to create a new word, message, or alphabet. (Take the first letter of the four cardinal directions, North, East, West, South, and you find the word NEWS, a promise of all-encompassing information from all directions.)
   In the scripture, certain writings intentionally emphasize acrostics. Each of the stanzas of Psalm 119 begins with a different Hebrew letter. Additional acrostics in the Psalms: Psalms 9 and 10, linked together. Psalm 25, 34, 37, 111, 112, 145. Also the first four chapters of Lamentations, and the description of the wife of noble character in Prov-erbs 31:10-31.

2 Deuteronomy 16

3 Apparently, only two other times in the scriptures, does God's name show up in acrostics of any sort: in Psalm 96:11, and in I Chronicles 16:31, which both use the same sentence: "Let the heavens rejoice, let the earth be glad!" Amen!

4 The internet puts this date at 721 BC. My reference works claim 611 BC.

5 The internet puts this date at 587 BC. My reference works claim 477 BC.

6 The NIV calls this city "Susa." The KJV calls it "Shushan."

7 Different scholars put these books in different orders. I am relying on the scholarship and notes of *The Companion Bible.*

8 Though scholars debate dates, the reference works I use claim Moses and Deuteronomy in 1452 BC, and the book of Esther from 472-422 BC.

9 Deuteronomy 31:16-18

10 Genesis 14:1 through the end of the chapter.

11 Ruth 1:1 through the end of the book.

12 II Samuel 21:1, through verse 14, quoted here.

13 Isaiah 7:1, through verse 17.

14 Jeremiah 1:3, through 1:19, quoted here.

15 Esther 1:1 (KJV)

16 *The Companion Bible*, p. 655.

17 Esther 1:8

18 In Daniel, he says the more familiar "Law of the Medes and the Persians." Esther reverses this order, except in 10:2.

19 Esther 1:15 (NIV), but with the edit from "King Xerxes" to "King Ahasuerus." The Hebrew manu-script uses the word "Ahasuerus."

20 Esther 1:16-18 (NIV), but with the edit from "King Xerxes" to "King Ahasuerus," in keeping with the Hebrew scriptures.

21 As in Song of Songs, the other book of the Bible with no outright mention of God's name.

22 *The Companion Bible*, Appendix 60, p. 85.

23 Esther 1:21-22

24 Esther 2:2-4

25 *The Companion Bible* notes that the generally received date, 598 BC, makes no sense. Their revised dating system puts the capture of Jehoiachin in 489 BC, and Astyages' marriage in his seventh year in 467. Thus, Mordecai had lived 22 years in Susa at that time.

26 Judges 21:25

27 Judges 21:1

28 Judges 21:3

29 Judges 21:21-22

30 Full shocking story in Judges 19-21

31 When the prophet Samuel first delivers the news to Saul that he will be king, Saul protests. "Saul answered, 'But am I not a Benjamite, from the smallest tribe of Israel, and is not my clan the least of all the clans of the tribe of Benjamin? Why do you say such a thing to me?'" (I Samuel 9:21)

32 II Samuel 16:5-14

33 II Samuel 19:16-23

34 I Kings 2:8-9

35 I Kings 2:36-46

36 Isaiah 55:12-13

37 Psalm 8:1-4

38 Esther 2:9 (KJV)

39 https://www.christianity.com/wiki/christian-terms/what-is-hesed-love-and-what-does-it-tell-us-about-gods-love-for-us.html. Found 4/6/2022.

40 Ibid.

41 https://www.compellingtruth.org/meaning-of-hesed.html. Found 4/6/2022.

42 https://firmisrael.org/learn/the-meaning-of-hesed-hebrew-for-love/. Found 4/6/2022.

43 Ibid, quoting Dr. Will Kynes.

44 Ibid, quoting Lois Tverberg.

45 Genesis 19:19

46 Zechariah 7:9

47 Micah 6:8

48 Psalm 23:6

49 https://www.blueletterbible.org/lexicon/h8034/kjv/wlc/0-1/. Found 2022.04.30.

50 From Exodus 34:6-7

51 Esther 2:11

52 *The Companion Bible*, note p. 656.

53 https://www.healthline.com/nutrition/myrrh-oil#TOC_TITLE_HDR_9. Found 4/7/2022.

54 Esther 2:14

55 Esther 2:15

56 Tebeth, January in the Western calendar

57 Esther 2:17

58 Esther 1:3 (KJV)

59 Esther 2:18 (KJV)

60 Proverbs 11:10

61 This phrase shows up twice: Esther 2:19, 21

62 https://goddidntsaythat.com/2014/03/11/was-haman-hanged-or-impaled-in-the-book-of-esther/. Found 4/13/2022.

63 https://www.ligonier.org/learn/articles/was-haman-hanged-or-impaled. Found 4/13/2022.

64 Esther 2:22

65 Malachi 1:2-3

66 Genesis 36:12

67 Exodus 17:8

68 Exodus 17:14-16 (KJV)

69 Exodus 17:14

70 Numbers 24:5

71 Numbers 24:20

72 Deuteronomy 25:17-19

73 Judges 3:13

74 Judges 5:14

75 I Samuel 15:2-3

76 I Samuel 15:10-11

77 I Samuel 15:22, 28

78 I Samuel 15:32-33

79 Rabbi Lapin, *Clash of Destiny* recording.

80 "Called an Amalekite by [ancient Jewish historian] Josephus (Ant. xi. 6. 5)." *The Companion Bible* note, p. 657.

81 Judges 5:27

82 I Samuel 4:19

83 I Kings 8:54

84 I Kings 19:18

85 Genesis 18:2

86 Exodus 20:5

87 Exodus 24:1

88 Judges 2:12 and others

89 *The Companion Bible*, p. 658.

90 Nisan, April in the Western calendar

91 Isaiah 47:12-15

92 Adar, March in the Western calendar

93 Esther 3:8-9

94 John 11:50

95 Acts 19:40

96 The NIV note on Esther 3:9 claims this is 375 tons of silver.

97 Calculation: 375 tons equals 750,000 pounds, or 10,937,500 troy ounces.

98 Exodus 30:11-16

99 Exodus 21:32. This is also the purchase price, of course, of Jesus, in Matthew 26:11.

100 http://www.bibleinsight.com/weights.html. Found 2022.04.30.

101 https://www.oxfordhandbooks.com/view/10.1093/oxford-hb/9780199935390.001.0001/oxford-hb-9780199935390-e-34. Found 2022.04.30.

102 As I understand it, this is the taxed income, and not the GDP.

103 Genesis 12:3

104 Esther 3:15

105 Joel 1:18

106 Exodus 14:3 (KJV)

107 I Peter 2:14

108 Proverbs 29:2

109 Esther 4:1-3

110 Psalm 22:1,19

111 Psalm 22:23

112 Esther 4:1

113 Esther 4:3

114 Isaiah 58:5

115 Jeremiah 6:26

116 Daniel 9:3

117 Jonah 3:6

118 Matthew 11:21

119 Luke 10:13

120 Esther 4:11

121 Esther 4:13-14

122 Esther 4:16

123 Esther 4:17

124 Esther 4:13-14

125 Jonah 3:4 (KJV)

126 Jonah 3:9

127 For this is what the Lord Almighty says: "After the Glorious One has sent me against the nations that have plundered you—for whoever touches you touches the apple of his eye" (Zechariah 2:8).

128 Esther 5:3

129 Exodus 4:1-2

130 The word can also imply the idea of a banquet.

131 *The Companion Bible*, Appendix 60, p. 86.

132 Esther 5:6

133 Esther 5:7-8

134 Esther 5:9

135 I Chronicles 16:31

136 Genesis 1:4

137 Esther 5:10-12

138 Esther 5:13

139 *The Companion Bible*, Appendix 60, p. 86.

140 23 meters

141 Esther 6:1

142 This is how Sight and Sound Theater's production of Esther reenacts this scene.

143 Luke 8:17

144 Proverbs 21:1 (NLT)

145 Esther 6:3

146 From Esther 6:4-6

147 Esther 6:6

148 From Esther 6:4-6

149 Esther 6:7-9

150 Esther 6:14

151 Esther 7:1

152 Esther 7:3-4

153 Esther 7:4

154 Note for Esther 7:4 NIV

155 Esther 7:4 KJV

156 Computer dictionary definition

157 Exodus 3:15

158 Exodus 3:14

159 "I will be what I will be": note for Exodus 3:14 NIV. "And write the story I will write." From a dinner conversation with Perry Marshall, based on his own reading of a Rabbi (Rabbi Jonathan, if I remember correctly), January 22, 2020.

160 Esther 7:6

161 Esther 7:7

162 Esther 7:7 KJV

163 *The Companion Bible*, Appendix 60, p. 86.

164 Esther 7:8

165 Esther 7:8

166 Deuteronomy 19:15

167 Esther 8:2

168 Esther 8:3-6

169 Sivan corresponds to May-June.

170 Esther 8:15-17

171 Esther 8:16

172 Hebrew Interlinear Bible. https://www.scripture4all.org/ OnlineInterlinear/OTpdf/est8.pdf. Found 4/16/2022.

173 Proverbs 1:7

174 Note in *The Passion Translation* for this verse.

175 Esther 8:15-17

176 Job 3:25

177 Genesis 12:3

178 Esther 9:4 KJV

179 Esther 9:5-6 KJV

180 I Samuel 15:3

181 I Samuel 15:19

182 Esther 9:10

183 From I Samuel 15:22

184 Esther 9:12

185 Esther 9:19

186 "Tradition has it that the core of the book was written by Mordechai, its main character and the cousin of Esther, and that the text was later redacted by the Great Assembly (a Jewish council of sages in antiquity)." https://www.haaretz.com/jewish/. premium-who-wrote-the-book-of-esther-1.5331950. Found 4/16/2022.

187 Esther 9:23-28, using the alternative translation in verse 25.

188 Esther 9:29-32, paraphrased from the NIV and various translations

189 Proverbs 16:33

190 Esther 10:2

191 Isaiah 49:6

192 A compilation of translations from https://biblehub.com/ esther/10-3.htm. Found 2022.04.16.

REFERENCES

Verse-by-Verse Analysis

King James Version

New International Version

Interlinear Bible:
https://www.scripture4all.org/OnlineInterlinear/Hebrew_Index.htm

The Companion Bible

BlueLetterBible.org

Additional Resources

The Bible Project
https://www.youtube.com/watch?v=JydNSlufRIs

Rabbi Lapin, *Clash of Destiny*

Sight and Sound Theater's *Esther*

ABOUT THE AUTHOR

A.J. Lykosh loves healing and deliverance.

Her heart's cry comes from the verse, "My people are destroyed for lack of knowledge" (Hosea 4:6). The author of several highly acclaimed books, she seeks to stop the destruction as best she can through writing and speaking. She sends daily emails about prayer, and podcasts at Make Prayer Beautiful.

She loves feedback. Email amy@workplaceprayer.com to start a conversation.

THE PRINCE PROTECTS HIS CITY
Nehemiah Prayed Four Months, Then Rebuilt the Wall in Only 52 Days

A free verse look at the book of Nehemiah. Come meet a man who brought God's kingdom to bear in his work. Nehemiah wasn't a warrior or a king. He was a tremendous administrator, a gifted leader, a world-class historian, a treasured friend, a successful fund-raiser, and a prince. And he prayed constantly.

"Loved it. Such a nice quick pace to read Nehemiah and also space to sit in parts if I just wanted to read one page" — **Angela**

FIND OUT MORE AT
amazon.com

ONE VOICE: THE STORY OF WILLIAM WILBERFORCE
Gorgeous Story of Tenacity + Courage

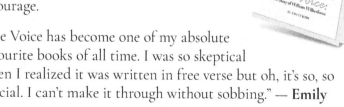

Biography in verse of the man who, despite all obstacles, fought to end the Slave Trade in Great Britain. Powerful story of tenacity and courage.

"One Voice has become one of my absolute favourite books of all time. I was so skeptical when I realized it was written in free verse but oh, it's so, so special. I can't make it through without sobbing." — **Emily**

FIND OUT MORE AT
sonlight.com

21 DAYS OF A F(E)AST
A Fast That Feels More Like a Feast

Why fasting is a joy, and why you should do it. A guide for a fast that anyone can do, even if you can't restrict calories. The four types of fasting, and how to choose. Morning and evening readings for 21 days. Stories and testimonies. Drawn from four decades of experience and wisdom. Come sit in the Lord's presence.

"Appreciating the wealth within this book!! Such a brilliant resource!" — **Nicole**

FIND OUT MORE AT
amazon.com

PRAYER REFRESH
Short Prayers to Pray Through Your Day

You don't have to completely change your life, your habits, your personality, or your social media usage in order to have a good prayer life. This book introduces a wide variety of prayers that you can pray in a minute or less, that will fit into your day, right where you are. Use it as a 21 day devotional, or read straight through.

"The Prayer Refresh was so life changing, perspective shattering, and breathed so much, much needed life into me and our home that I long to go through it again. Regularly. Like monthly." — **Amanda**

FIND OUT MORE AT
amazon.com

JUNETEENTH: AN INVITATION TO FAST
Both the Why and the How To

Join us in a one-day fast. In Christ alone do we find peace, forgiveness, reconciliation, and restoration. Because we want more of these, we offer an invitation to fast on Juneteenth.

"The booklet was so helpful with the historical summary of the date (which I knew nothing about), as well as specific prayers and family examples, to guide my focused petitions. The format is beautiful, and so clearly organized! Great resource!" — **Eileen**

FIND OUT MORE AT
amazon.com

GROW WITH PRAYER EXPERIENCES

Throughout the year, we offer a wide range of prayer experiences: Communal Fasts, Prayer Challenges, and Sacred Assemblies.

If you want to grow in prayer in creative and unexpected ways, come join us.

FIND OUT MORE AT
PrayerExperiences.com

Made in the USA
Monee, IL
27 October 2022